D1084579

Will they do it again?

Focus in the media on the risks posed to ordinary people has become increasingly strong in recent years – particularly on those risks popularly perceived to be posed by the mentally disordered. But how justified is this concern? How do we best manage so-called dangerous people?

In *Will they do it again?* Herschel Prins considers the issue of public protection within a broad context of risk in society generally, examining the concerns arising in contemporary society from dealing with uncertainty. It is argued that public fear over the danger posed by the mentally disordered is at odds with the evidence, and that much of the concern is focused on a small number of high-profile cases. Prins goes on to examine such cases where their management has failed and sets out suggestions for improvements in practice.

Will they do it again? cuts through popular misunderstanding and media hype over risk to give a clear, unbiased picture of the real risks to society from the mentally disordered and how best they can be contained and managed; it will prove invaluable to a range of practitioners involved in the fields of criminal justice, psychiatry and psychology.

Herschel Prins is a Professor at the Midlands Centre for Criminology and Criminal Justice at the University of Loughborough and Visiting Professor, Nottingham Trent University.

Will they do it again?

Risk assessment and management
in criminal justice and psychiatry

Herschel Prins

Foreword by
Professor Keith Soothill

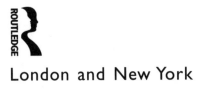

London and New York

First published 1999 by Routledge
11 New Fetter Lane, London EC4P 4EE

Simultaneously published in the USA and Canada by Routledge
29 West 35th Street, New York, NY 10001

© 1999 Herschel Prins

Typeset in Times by Graphicraft Limited, Hong Kong
Printed and bound in Great Britain by TJ International Ltd, Padstow,
Cornwall

British Library Cataloguing in Publication Data
A catalogue record for this book is available from
the British Library

Library of Congress Cataloging in Publication Data

ISBN 0–415–16017–0 (hbk)
ISBN 0–415–16018–9 (pbk)

This book is dedicated to all who have been my students and who have helped me to a greater understanding of some of the issues described and discussed herein.

When once the itch of literature comes over man, nothing can cure it but the scratching of a pen.

Samuel Lover, *Handy Andy*

Contents

Tables

Foreword

When John Milton wrote over three hundred years ago in *Paradise Lost* (1667) that 'Chance governs all' (2, 910), he could not have imagined how such concepts as 'chance' and 'risk' would take centre stage in modern society. Ulrich Beck has famously embraced the notion of The Risk Society and a rather bold assumption that life used to be secure, but now it is full of risks. More prosaically, a high proportion of the British population seem to place their hopes of financial salvation on winning the National Lottery, but there is little risk of that happening with its one-in-14 million chance of success. 'Chance' and 'risk' are pervasive, but there is a wide range of contexts from the trivial to the serious in which these concepts are used.

Widely publicised deaths where members of the public have been killed by recently released psychiatric patients or by grossly disturbed offenders have brought home the point that those concerned with risk assessment and management within the criminal justice and mental health systems are engaged in a hazardous business. No one can deny that the subject area of this book is important. In fact, this 'business' has turned into a 'risk *industry*' with many persons finding a niche in this seemingly new market. However, neither the issues nor the problems are new. We have always had to deal with dangerous people. So what can yet another book on the subject tell us that is worth hearing?

I have known of Herschel Prins's work for a long time but we have rarely met. Some other readers of my age may have a similar relationship with Herschel. We have perhaps come to expect at least three qualities in his books which wonderfully mesh together. First, he has a very special talent for making convoluted and tortured topics clear. Clarity rarely enhances one's academic reputation, for there is little left to argue about. Clarity, however, appeals to readers, for they can begin to understand a subject which the experts have begun to claim. Secondly, his scholarship is impressive. His reading embraces legal, psychiatric and sociological sources, but literature, both ancient and modern, comes within his range. A recent quotation from the *Royal Society* opens the book and one from Shakespeare's *Macbeth* concludes its argument. Which provides the greater insight, you can judge. Thirdly, his experience is telling. In various ways Herschel Prins has been involved in the areas of criminal justice and mental health for nearly fifty years and more directly in the 'risk industry' for the past fifteen years or so. He has chaired or been a panel member on various relevant inquiries and, more recently, has been the chair of NACRO's Mental Health Advisory Committee which produced an important report last year entitled *Risk and rights: Mentally disturbed offenders and public protection*. No one could be in a better position to produce a book on risk assessment and management in criminal justice and psychiatry. So what does clarity, scholarship and experience produce?

This is not a technical book produced by a young technocrat trying to persuade us that a new technique provides the answer to risk assessment. This book reminds us there is no quick fix – indeed, 'the aim of this book . . . is to suggest that there is no magic or philosopher's stone in this area of work' (p. 138). He appeals more to the tradition of which the late Dr Peter Scott was the doyen 'of taking the thoughtful time-centred rounded view' (p. 134). However, this is not a complacent book, for Prins identifies, for example, that 'we still have a long way to go in encouraging mental health and criminal justice professionals to take a broad view of an individual's social functioning in relation to their illness' (p. 104) and that 'changes are required in the present system of inquiries' (p. 110). Change will not come easily. Meanwhile, his suggestions in the last chapter on 'Improving practice' focus on issues which can be addressed.

Keith Soothill
Professor of Social Research
Lancaster University
January 1999

Preface

For reasons set out in the first chapter of this book, risk assessment and management have become major issues of concern during the past decade. In pursuance of this concern (and maybe to capitalise on it) a number of very useful books have appeared in recent times. Examples are: Adams (1995), Duggan (1997), Kemshall (1996), Kemshall and Pritchard (1996; 1997), McMurran and Hodge (1994), Moore (1996), Royal Society (1992), Vincent (1995), Walker (1996) and Webster et al. (1994). Intending readers of this volume may well ask, why add another work to this already considerable literature? My reasons (at least at a conscious level) are two-fold. First, to my regret, this book has been over-long in its gestation with the result that other works have appeared, and may to some extent have overtaken it. The second reason is that despite the existence of the aforementioned works, I consider that there is still room for a book that combines specialist treatment of the topic with an attempt to place such specialist treatment within a broader conceptual context of risk in modern society.

Some further words of explanation are necessary. This book is concerned predominantly with the commission of harmful (violent) behaviour towards others and the prevention of its repetition. I acknowledge that in a number of cases the perpetration of serious violence arises without obvious warning; most of the cases I am concerned with are those in which violence has already been committed. Two further disclaimers are necessary. First, this book does not deal with harm towards self though, as will become clear, many of the approaches that are helpful in limiting harm to others are also capable of extension to harm to self. Second, this book is not *specifically* concerned with dangerous behaviours in the workplace and how they may be avoided; these can perhaps be best described as the 'health, safety and welfare' aspects of the problem. Having said this, I acknowledge that some of the individuals described in this book may also present harmful behaviours in offices and similar locations.

The following topics are covered in the book: risk and risk-taking in society; legal and administrative aspects of risk-taking in criminal justice and mental health; the role of mental disorders in relation to risk; learning lessons (the place of public and private inquiries); clinical risk assessment and management; improving skills. In previous works I have made suggestions for further reading. I have not done so on this occasion as the notes and references to each chapter offer guidance for those who wish to develop their knowledge beyond the inevitable limitations of a short text. The notes and references, therefore, should not be viewed as academic pretension on my part.

REFERENCES

Adams, J. (1995). *Risk*. London: University College London Press.

Duggan, C. (ed.). (1997). Assessing risk in the mentally disordered. *British Journal of Psychiatry*, 170 (Suppl. 32).

Kemshall, H. (1996). *Reviewing risk: A review of research on the assessment and management of risk and dangerousness: Implications for policy and practice in the probation service*. London: Home Office.

Kemshall, H., & Pritchard, J. (eds). (1996). *Good practice in risk assessment and management* (Vol. 1). London: Jessica Kingsley.

Kemshall, H., & Pritchard, J. (1997). *Good practice in risk assessment and management* (Vol. 2). London: Jessica Kingsley.

McMurran, M., & Hodge, J. (eds). (1994). *The assessment of criminal behaviours of clients in secure settings*. London: Jessica Kingsley.

Moore, B. (1996). *Risk assessment: A practitioner's guide to predicting harmful behaviours*. London: Whiting and Birch.

Royal Society. (1992). *Risk: Analysis, perception, management: Report of the Royal Society study group*. London: Author.

Vincent, C. (ed.). (1995). *Clinical risk management*. London: BMJ Publishing Group.

Walker, N. (ed.). (1996). *Dangerous people*. London: Blackstone Press.

Webster, C.D., Harris, G.T., Rice, M.E., Cormier, C., & Quinsey, V.L. (1994). *The violence prediction scheme: Assessing dangerousness in high risk men*. Toronto: Centre of Criminology, University of Toronto.

Acknowledgements

My warmest appreciation is extended to my two editorial mentors at Routledge – first, over many years, Edwina Welham, and more recently, Kate Hawes. They have been most patient and courteous in accepting considerable delays on my part in meeting the deadline for this book. A considerable proportion of the material contained in the following pages has been used and discussed over the years at numerous workshops and conferences; my thanks to all those participants who shared their experiences with me and deepened my understanding of the nature of risk. I would like to express my very warm thanks to Mike Todd, Chief Executive of the Parole Board, Nigel Shackleford and Mike Boyle of the Mental Health Unit of the Home Office, Ms Gill Mckenzie, Chief Probation Officer for Gloucestershire and to my colleague Professor Keith Soothill of Lancaster University for reading the final version of the manuscript and for so kindly writing the Foreword.

Thanks are also due to the following for permission to quote from or reproduce copyright material: Her Majesty's Stationery Office and Gloucestershire Probation Service for permission to reproduce the material that appears as Appendices to Chapter 5.

Once again my gratitude must be expressed to Janet Kirkwood for working the usual miracles on her word processor, turning my untidy drafts into pristine examples of the written word. Finally, my heartfelt thanks to my wife, Norma, who has, as always, borne patiently with me during the preparation of the book; her careful reading of every word has prevented many errors and infelicities in presentation. Any errors that remain are my responsibility.

Herschel Prins
Houghton on the Hill
Leicestershire, 1999

Note on case examples

Where cases have been quoted by way of illustration, essential identifying data have been removed in order to preserve anonymity; in some cases, composite presentations have been constructed. Cases that have been in the public domain are quoted without the above alterations.

Chapter 1

Understanding uncertainty

Risk is ubiquitous and no human activity can be considered risk free.

Royal Society, *Risk*

Giddens states that 'A risk Society is a Society where we can increasingly live on a high technological frontier which absolutely no-one completely understands and which generates a diversity of possible futures' (in Franklin, 1998: 25). Much recent writing about risk seems to centre around the problem identified by Giddens, namely the reconciliation of advances in the boundaries of knowledge and invention on the one hand, and coping with the inevitable ambiguities and uncertainties that such developments create on the other. One thing is very clear: humankind[1] abhors ambiguity and uncertainty; humans will engage in dubious and sometimes harmful practices to avoid them. Much recent and current concern about 'dangerous' people has its roots in these phenomena; unless they are properly understood many of our efforts aimed at dealing with such people will fail. Ulrich Beck puts an eloquent gloss on the matter. He highlights the fact that what he describes as 'manufactured uncertainty . . . has become an inescapable part of our lives and everybody is facing unknown and barely calculable risks'. He continues:

Calculating and managing risks which nobody really knows has become one of our main preoccupations. That used to be a specialist job for actuaries, insurers and scientists. Now, we all have to engage in it, with whatever rusty tools we can lay our hands on – sometimes the calculator, sometimes the astrology column.

(Beck in Franklin, 1998: 12)

In modern society, politicians are frequently answerable for the activities of the experts Beck refers to, over whom they have little control and even less knowledge. For this reason professional decision makers should not fall into the trap of encouraging the public to think that they can be protected from all forms of risk. This is of considerable importance in the area of criminal justice and mental health. An analogy drawn from psychiatry as practised in the 1950s and early 1960s may help to make my point clear. At that time, some psychiatrists were rather over-optimistic about the degree to which, armed with recently developed drugs, they could provide effective remedies for mental illness. A degree of initial success on their part, created in the minds of the public the notion that maybe psychiatry could effectively deal with other forms of human malaise or, as Szasz suggested, in problems of living (Szasz, 1987). Such expectations were premature and many psychiatrists were to regret later having gone along with these expectations. That they did so was not necessarily due to arrogance on their part, but rather to a degree of over-optimism that psychiatry might have the answers to problems beyond its realistic professional remit. Today, criminal justice and mental health practitioners stand in danger of perpetrating the same errors. This matter is dealt with in more detail in Chapter 5. Anna Coote (1998) has some sensible advice to offer those engaged in the risk business. She suggests that:

> . . . we must become skilled at planning for uncertainty. We no longer rely on scientific expertise or economics to predict with any certainty how things will turn out in the future . . . we must be clear about what we do know and where we really are at present. Planning for uncertainty involves a realistic appraisal of the evidence at our disposal, a deep understanding of the present (not marred by a rose-tinted view of the past).
>
> (Coote, in Franklin, 1998: 129–130)

Beck (1997)[2] adds emphasis to this view:

> Risk Society begins where tradition ends, when, in all spheres of life, we can no longer take traditional certainties for granted. The less we can rely on traditional securities, the more risks we have to negotiate. The more risk, the more decisions and choices we have to make.
>
> (Beck, 1997: 4)

All this supports the contention that, as the writer Sara Maitland says:

Life is a risky business . . . We are weak and vulnerable and even virtue may not protect us ultimately. Things are not what they seem and may change at any moment, change without human cause . . . but underneath all this peril there is also a safety; truth and order will somehow be restored.

(Maitland, 1997)

PUBLIC PERCEPTIONS OF RISK

Where scientific fact falls short of certainty we are guided by assumption, inference and belief.

Adams, 1995

Risk perception is very much an individual matter. A highly sensitive account of how parents perceive risk is that given by Blake Morrison in his book about the Bulger case, *As If* (1997). Morrison not only covered the trial in detail but also immersed himself in the local scene. In addition, he related his reactions to the trial to his own experiences as husband and father. He writes perceptively about what he describes as the risks of childhood and parents' fears of childhood disasters; for example, drowning, being run over, murdered, over-lain, cot-death, meningitis, electrocution, fall from a great height, drinking bleach, dying by fire, killed by an animal, in an aeroplane disaster, then, as an adult (but still in the eyes of parents *as a child*) killed in a car crash, in a flying or shooting accident. The hazards and their accompanying irrational fears seem endless.

Media images of risk

Most of the general public's fears about risk are generated through the media. A leader in the *Independent* of 13 July 1996 p. 15 expresses this admirably:

It has been a murderously bad year for the children of England. In a green Kentish lane, a mother, her children and the family pet are set upon. Such was the ferocity of the attack the police labelled the killer 'deranged'. In the urban West Midlands a man with a machete invades a primary school picnic . . . teddy bears piled in a corner where terrified children abandoned them as they fled . . . on Merseyside, a child's body discovered and a perpetrator sought amid echoes of the Bulger case.

From such quotes, we may be led to assume that the modern techno-
logically sophisticated world is a place quite unfit for our children (and,
for that matter, adults) to live in. The media influence is pervasive and
damaging to human relations and experience, particularly for children.
The numbers of children taxied to school by their worried parents
has increased enormously. In 1971, 80 per cent of seven- and eight-
year-olds were going to school alone; today, it is suggested that fewer
than 10 per cent do so (*Independent*, 22 July 1996, p. 11). As I write
this chapter, teachers are expressing a reluctance to protect their small
charges from the harmful rays of the sun with barrier creams for fear of
being accused of sexual or physical molestation.

However, life has always been full of hazards: we lose our sense of
perspective on this at our peril. It is salutary to remind ourselves of the
seventeenth-century philosopher Thomas Hobbes: 'No arts; no letters;
no society; and which is worst of all, continual fear and danger of
violent death; and the life of man, solitary, poor, nasty, brutish and
short' (*Leviathan*, Pt.i, 13). One could find many more examples of
what sociological criminologists such as Cohen once described as 'moral
panics' (Cohen, 1972). A moral panic 'is not another way of defining
mass hysteria, rather it is a technical term to describe social movements
that define a variety of actions, groups or persons as a (serious) threat to
fundamental social values' (La Fontaine, 1998: 19).[3]

Obtaining a sense of proportion

The following are some facts drawn from various more responsible
newspaper accounts of some of life's *real* hazards.

Writing about some of the realities of risk, a leader writer in the
Independent of 22 July 1996, p. 11 suggested that:

> walking was (more) dangerous than cycling, which is more dan-
> gerous than travelling by car, which is far more dangerous than
> flying . . . in spite of Dunblane and similar incidents, children are
> still safer in the classroom than in the home. . . . and they are less
> at risk from strangers than from parents.

It is worth noting that the child murder rate has remained much the
same over the last two decades: eighty-five or so children murdered
each year, most of them infants killed by parents.

Despite the truth of these statements it has proved, for example, well nigh impossible to convince many parents that there are more unidentified paedophiles at large in the community than those whose identity is known and who have recently been released from prison.

Similar considerations apply to those individuals known to the psychiatric services who have committed homicide. As we shall see later, their numbers remain fairly stable over time and are very small in comparison to the total number of homicides committed each year. However, such statistics do nothing to dispel the images held by the public of the axe-wielding schizophrenic.

Despite these concerns, people do seem to find ways of putting beyond their immediate comprehension a variety of possible hazardous events. For example, despite the awesome catalogue of IRA outrages, people continued to travel to work in high risk areas, and a great many people did not take very long to return to eating beef following the initial scares about BSE. As the leader writer quoted earlier went on to say, 'the idea that the department store we are about to walk into could explode around us is almost inconceivable, so is the notion that the tasty steak in front of us could turn our brains to jelly'. But, as the writer concluded, 'where children are concerned we can imagine the dangers only too well . . . present us with a story about a battered child and rationality deserts us'.

Some hazardous events

The following table gives an indication of the likelihood of our meeting a hazardous event.

Hartston (in the *Independent Magazine*, 19 September 1997, pp. 10–11) gives a somewhat humorous, but none the less highly perceptive account of modern risk taking:

> Such are the risks we all run every day that, if you are an adult aged between 35 and 54, there is roughly a one-in-400 chance you will be dead within a year. *Homo sapiens* is a bit of a twit about assessing risks. We buy lottery tickets in the hope of scooping the jackpot, with a one-in-14 million chance of winning, when there's a one-in-400 chance that we won't even survive the year . . . the evidence suggests that our behaviour is motivated by panic and innumeracy.

Hartston attempts to place all of this into perspective:

Table 1.1 Likelihood of involvement in a hazardous event

Contracting CJD by eating 'beef on the bone'	one in 6 million
Being struck by lightning	one in 10 million
Drowning in the bath	one in 800,000
Death from homicide	one in 100,000
Death playing soccer	one in 25,000
Dying in a plane crash	one in 20,000
Dying from being involved in a road accident	one in 8,000
Dying from 'flu	one in 5,000
Dying from smoking ten cigarettes a day	one in 200

Source: *Daily Telegraph*, 5 December 1997, p. 9.

Notes

a Compared with the risk of death from eating beef on the bone, the other risks quoted are far more substantial; as the author of the article from which these figures are extrapolated states, the risk is 'so small that it almost tips off the scale' (R. Uhlig, *Daily Telegraph*, 5 December 1997).

b Statistical odds may be expressed in the following fashion:

Negligible risk is	less than one in 1,000,000
Minimal risk is	one in 100,000 to one in 1,000,000
Very low risk is	one in 10,000 to one in 100,000
Low risk is	one in 1,000 to one in 10,000
Moderate risk is	one in 100 to one in 1,000
High risk is	greater than one in 100.

Source: Sir Kenneth Calman, Former Chief Medical Officer of Health, Department of Health, as quoted in *The Guardian*, 3 October 1996, p. 6.

> *One death equals*
> 10 million flights on a jet aeroplane
> 75 million trains boarded
> 200 million baths taken
> 4 million cycle trips
> 500 million staircases climbed
> 3 million acts of unprotected sex
> 200 million roads crossed
> 15 million car journeys
> 2 million cigarettes smoked

In concluding his article Hartston states, 'However safe or dangerous the environment may be, we all settle for a level of risk taking that keeps life as dangerous as we want it.'

Such perceptions of risk have very important implications. Measures taken to reduce risks may have unseen (and sometimes hazardous) consequences. For example, as Hartston suggests, 'there is considerable evidence that wearing seat belts makes drivers more reckless because they feel safer'; and 'Marking a road as an "accident black spot" may reduce accident figures so successfully that it ceases to be a black spot – it was only dangerous in the first place because people didn't realise how dangerous it was.' An example drawn from earlier times supports such contentions. Adams cites the introduction of the Davy Lamp which was intended to save lives in the mining industry; but as Adams suggests, it actually resulted in an *increase* in explosions and fatalities because the lamp permitted mining activity to be carried out at deeper levels where the explosive methane content was much higher (Adams, 1995: 211).

PROFESSIONAL PERCEPTIONS OF RISKS

There can be little doubt that there has been a massive growth in what can best be called the 'risk industry'. This is exemplified in concerns about safety in the home, safety at work, the development of casualty services and those associated with road, rail and sea accidents.

Adams (1995) suggests that we may all tend to overdo the risk-prevention business. He cites as examples, over-estimates of household risks which lead to unnecessary expenditure on insurance; the design of buildings which take into account hazards which can be rated as almost zero, such as earthquakes in areas where these are unlikely; over-zealous safety measures on the railways leading to increases in passenger costs which, in turn, may drive people away from the railways on to the roads, thus creating greater driving hazards; abnormal fears of mugging and similar attacks may lead the elderly and other vulnerable people to lead unnecessarily isolated lives. Adams suggests that there are two types of human. The first is zero-risk man *homo prudens*, personifying 'prudence, rationality and responsibility' (p. 17). He describes this creature as 'a figment of the imagination of the safety profession'. The second is a type of being within every one of us, a creature he describes as *homo aleatorius*: 'dice man, gambling man, risk-taking man'. He suggests that the latter is much nearer to the true nature of man; his descriptions give further credibility to the importance of *irrationality* in human risk-taking behaviour or abstention from it.

Definitions of risk

In 1983, The Royal Society produced a report on *Risk*. This was subsequently revised in the light of developments in knowledge and practice and a further version appeared in 1992 (Royal Society, 1992). In their introduction to this later report, the authors concentrated their minds on a range of terms used in the literature on risk. Some of them are quoted below:

- *Risk* is defined in terms of the probability 'that a particular adverse event occurs during a stated period of time, or results from a particular challenge' (p. 2).[4]
- A *hazard* is defined as 'the situation that in particular circumstances could lead to harm . . .' (p. 3).
- *Risk Assessment* is used to 'describe the study of decisions subject to uncertain consequences' (p. 3).[5] The Royal Society working group divided risk assessment into *risk estimation* and *risk evaluation*.
- *Risk Estimation* 'includes: (a) the identification of the outcomes; (b) the estimation of the magnitude of the associated consequences of these outcomes; and (c) the estimation of the probabilities of these outcomes' (p. 3).
- *Risk Evaluation* is 'the complex process of determining the significance or value of the identified hazards and estimated risks to those concerned with or affected by the decision' (p. 3).
- *Risk Management* is 'the making of decisions concerning risks and their subsequent implementation, and flows from risk estimation and risk evaluation' (p. 3).

The authors of the report cautioned against equating *risk* with *danger*. To put it simply, *risk* may be seen as the probability of an event occurring, and *danger* may be seen as the extent of the hazard or harm likely to accrue. The term 'acceptable risk' is frequently used by decision takers and policy makers. The authors of the Royal Society Report, supporting the views expressed by Layfield in his report on the Sizewell B nuclear plant inquiry, prefer the term 'tolerable'. Layfield considered that the use of the term 'acceptable' did not reflect the seriousness of the problems involved in risk-taking activities; he suggested the term 'tolerable' as being a more accurate description of what was involved. Following Layfield's report, the Health and Safety Executive defined 'tolerable risk' in the following fashion:

> 'Tolerability' does not mean 'acceptability'. It refers to the willingness to live with a risk to secure certain benefits and in the confidence that it is being properly controlled. To tolerate a risk means that we do not regard it as negligible or something we might

ignore, but rather as something we need to keep under review and reduce still further if and as we can.

(Quoted in Royal Society, 1992)

CONCLUSION

The aim of this chapter has been to provide a broad overview of some aspects of the phenomena of risk and risk taking in our society. I hope it will have become clear that views about risks and their impact owe much more to irrationality than to fact. It seems that, for whatever reasons, we have a need to create our own nightmares. This being the case, it is incumbent on the professionals involved in risk taking in criminal justice and mental health to be aware of this inimical factor as it is likely to have a profound influence on the manner in which they carry out their work. They also need to develop precision in their deployment of the terms used in assessing and managing risk.

The remainder of this book moves away from these more general issues and is devoted more specifically to risk assessment and management within criminal justice and mental health; however, some of the general issues broached in this chapter will be returned to in more detail. A final word of explanation is necessary: the division of the rest of the material in the book is somewhat arbitrary and a degree of overlap inevitable in an attempt to provide continuity.

NOTES

1 Throughout this book, generic terms for women and men are used, except where to do so would make for clumsy presentation.

2 For a long time Beck has been a key proponent of the notion of The Risk Society. This is said to be predicated on the assumptions that (1) there used to be social control over technology, but this has now disappeared, and that (2) life used to be secure; now it is full of risks. However, writers such as Steuer claim that many of Beck's assumptions are unproven (see Steuer, 1998).

3 La Fontaine's analysis of the phenomena of so-called satanic sexual abuse of children provides a sophisticated and methodologically very sound account of media-fed panics. An earlier and complementary account may be found in Soothill and Walby's systematic analysis of newspaper coverage of sex crimes. Based on some 5,000 newspapers from 40 years of newspaper coverage it indicates the extent to which such crimes are sometimes reported in a

misleading and trivialising fashion leading to sensationalist accounts. (Soothill & Walby, 1991). However, in a later contribution, Soothill (*The Guardian*, 13 January 1998, p. 17) suggests that a degree of discrimination is necessary in ascribing blame to the media:

> While many of us are ready to blame the media for most things, we need to be clearer what offence we are convicting them of. In relation to rape, for example, they currently over-emphasise severe sentences while failing to tell us about the extraordinarily high number of acquittals taking place in the courts. We do get a distorted message, but we need to understand more fully the nature of the distortion.

In a later more general survey of risk, Adams (1995) analysed the contents of two broadsheet and four tabloid newspapers for one day (28 January 1994). He found news accounts full of risk stories; the health pages contained no less than eleven, and even the gardening pages were concerned with the estimation of risks to various plants.

4 It is worth noting two comparable definitions from the disciplines of law and criminal justice. Carson, an academic lawyer with a keen interest in risk-taking behaviours, defines risk as 'a course of action or *inaction*, [emphasis added] taken under conditions of uncertainty, which exposes one to possible loss in order to reach a desired outcome' (Carson, 1995: 75). Kemshall, an academic in the field of criminal justice with a special interest in the risks managed by probation officers in dealing with serious offenders, states that 'risk is best understood as an uncertain prediction about future behaviour, with a chance that the future outcome of the behaviour will be harmful or negative' (Kemshall 1996: v).

5 Defined by Kemshall (1996: v) as 'a probability calculation that a harmful behaviour or event will occur and involves an assessment about the frequency of the behaviour/event, its likely impact and who it will affect'.

REFERENCES

Adams, J. (1995). *Risk*. London: University College London Press.

Beck, U. (1997). A risky business, *London School of Economics Magazine, 10*, 15–16.

Beck, U. (1998). Politics of risk society. In J. Franklin (ed.), *The politics of risk society*. Cambridge: Polity Press.

Carson, D. (1995). From risk assessment to risk management. In J. Braggins & C. Martin (eds), *Managing risk: Achieving the possible*. London: Institute for the Study and Treatment of Delinquency.

Cohen, S. (1972). *Folk devils and moral panics*. London: McGibbon and Kee.

Coote, A. (1998). Risk and public policy: Towards a high-trust democracy. In J. Franklin (ed.), *The politics of risk society*. Cambridge: Polity Press.

Giddens, A. (1998). Risk society: The context of British politics'. In J. Franklin (ed.), *The politics of risk society*. Cambridge: Polity Press.

Health and Safety Executive. (1988). *The tolerability of risks from nuclear power stations*. London: HMSO.

Kemshall, H. (1996). *Reviewing risk*. London: Home Office.

La Fontaine, J.S. (1998). *Speak of the devil: Tales of satanic abuse in contemporary England*. Cambridge: Cambridge University Press.

Maitland, S. (1997). Commentary in programme notes for Shakespeare's *Cymbeline*, 7 June 1997 Stratford-upon-Avon: Royal Shakespeare Company.

Morrison, B. (1997). *As If*. London: Granta Books.

Royal Society. (1992). *Risk: Analysis, perception, management*. London: Author.

Soothill, K., & Walby, S. (1991). *Sex crimes in the news*. London: Routledge.

Steuer, M. (1998). A little too risky. *London School of Economics Magazine*, *10*, 15–16.

Szasz, T. (1987). *Insanity: The idea and its consequences*. Chichester: Wiley.

Chapter 2

Legal and administrative aspects

The greater the power, the more dangerous the abuse.
Edmund Burke House of Commons, 7 February 1771

In this chapter I give an account of the background and current context to legislation and administrative procedures relating to those offenders and offender–patients considered to be at serious risk to others. Those wishing to acquaint (or re-acquaint) themselves with some of the more general aspects of mental health provision should consult Chapter 3 in Prins (1995a).[1]

BACKGROUND

Although the terms 'danger' and 'dangerousness' are not much favoured by professionals today (see also Chapter 1), the terms continue to be used in various jurisdictions and in common parlance.[2] A number of jurisdictions, notably in some of the states on the continent of North America, have made attempts to define dangerousness for the purpose of incarceration of those individuals adjudged to be dangerous, be this incarceration in penal or mental health care institutions. Currently in the UK, there are no statutes that attempt to define dangerous individuals specifically though the law does recognise such offences as reckless (dangerous) driving, endangering the lives of passengers, and in being in possession of, or distributing, dangerous drugs. However, as I shall show shortly, the notion of dangerousness has in recent times been an important consideration in criminal justice and mental health legislation. It is also of interest to note that in the last few years there has been an increase in the use of the 'life' (indeterminate) sentence for cases not involving homicide. In various UK Court of Appeal decisions this has been justified on the grounds that by such means offenders considered to be dangerous, but not meeting the criteria for detention under current mental health legislation, can be incarcerated until such time as the authorities (for example, the Home Secretary) consider, on the basis of expert opinion, that they can safely be released. However, we should note that decisions based on considerations of dangerousness seem to have recently become contaminated by considerations based on political expedience, as appears to have occurred in the case of Myra Hindley and some others.[3]

So far as those adjudged to be mentally disordered are concerned, current mental health legislation in England and Wales recognises the concept of potential dangerousness. Thus, Sections 2 and 3 of the 1983 Mental Health Act make provision, *inter alia*, for the compulsory detention of an individual with a view to the 'protection of other persons'.[4] The protection of others is also reflected in the Mental Health (Patients in the Community) Act 1995; this makes provision for dealing with a small group of seriously mentally ill persons in the community, thought to be a danger not only to themselves, but also *to others*. In recent times, case registration has become an important element in mental health care. Registration is to be applied to those suffering enduring mental illness and who are considered to be a danger to themselves and *to others*. However, as I have pointed out elsewhere (Prins, 1995b), there is nothing new about registers of one kind or another. Registration has its advocates and its detractors. Those in favour consider that such registration will enable problematic cases to be identified and tracked more easily; in addition, they suggest that registration will make it easier to attach funds to each case. Others have pointed to the disadvantages of stigma; to the possibility of mental health professionals being held legally accountable if they did *not* register a patient and that patient then committed a serious offence, such as homicide. Other concerns have centred upon inadequate definitions of severe and enduring mental illness (and of personality and psychopathic disorder, which are included). Further concerns focus on the point at which registration takes place and, of equal importance, the point of de-registration. In surveying these problems, limited comparisons can be made with registration practices in child care and probation. Little and Gibbons (1993) concluded, after a fairly comprehensive survey of the topic, that cases placed on the child care registers received significantly more services than those which were not registered, but despite this 'We must not therefore, treat registers as valid measures of child abuse and neglect.' (Little & Gibbons, 1993:

18). Probation services have maintained registers of 'high risk' offenders for some years. Both Shaw (1991) and the Home Office (1995) noted wide variations in registration practice and a degree of arbitrariness as to who should be included in such registers. As Inch et al. (1995: 168) state:

> Filling in forms or conducting questionnaires may create the impression that something is being done, but, at the same time no amount of such form filling will (assist) . . . if the fundamental causes are not tackled.

Section 41 of the 1983 Act makes provision (subject to certain strict criteria being satisfied) for placing an order restricting discharge on a person made the subject of a Hospital Order in order to protect the public from 'serious harm'.[5] More specifically, the proclivities of some patients and offender–patients are recognised in the setting up and maintenance of the three Special Hospitals in England and Wales (Broadmoor, Rampton and Ashworth) for those patients who 'exhibit dangerous, violent or criminal propensities' (National Health Service Act 1977, Section 4).[6] The law and practice relating to mentally abnormal, dangerous and potentially dangerous offenders, and now mentally abnormal offenders, have been examined by a number of bodies in recent years; for example, the Butler Committee, the Scottish Council on Crime, the Floud Committee and the Joint Department of Health and Home Office Committee, chaired by Dr John Reed.

The Butler Committee

The Butler Committee (Home Office & DHSS, 1975) made four important recommendations in relation to dangerousness. *First*, they proposed that a new form of sentence should be introduced from which release would be dependent entirely on the issues of dangerousness.[7] Such a sentence would be for offenders who were dangerous and who presented a history of mental disorder, but who could not be dealt with under the mental health legislation and for whom the life sentence was not considered to be appropriate (see above). Such a new sentence would be reviewable at two-yearly intervals; following discharge, the offender would be under statutory supervision. *Second*, the imposition of such a sentence would be restricted to those convicted of offences which caused, or might cause, harm to others; these would include such offences as murder, manslaughter, serious sexual offences, arson, grievous bodily harm with intent, robbery, aggravated burglary and certain other serious crimes. *Third*, the Home Secretary would have power to transfer prisoners serving a reviewable sentence from prison to hospital under the mental health legislation if their mental state warranted this, but a restriction would be placed on such an offender–patient's discharge. *Fourth*, the two-year review would be carried out by the Parole Board; release would be on licence of unlimited duration; however, the conditions of the licence would be subject to a two-yearly review with the possibility of eventual removal. As I shall show shortly, although these recommendations have not been carried through in the way the Butler Committee envisaged, recent criminal justice and mental health legislation has gone *some* way to implementing them.

The Scottish Council on Crime

In the same year, the Scottish Council on Crime (1975) recommended a new form of sentence – a 'public protection order'. This was designed for the offender prone to violence. The Council envisaged that this type of sentence would enable such offenders to be detained until it was safe for them to be released into the community.

The Floud Report

In 1976, The Howard League For Penal Reform convened a working party under the chairmanship of Mrs Jean Floud (then Principal of Newnham College, Cambridge) to consider the law and practice in relation to dangerous offenders. A report was produced in 1981 in which the working party concluded that the sentencing of dangerous offenders should be the subject of specific special legislation and that, subject to various safeguards, 'the public should be entitled to the protection of a special sentence only against grave harm' (Floud & Young, 1981: 154). 'Grave harm' included some of the offences falling within the Butler definition. The members of the working party were concerned that an offender's suitability for a mental health disposal should first be excluded before their new protective sentence could be imposed.

The Reed Review

In December 1990, The Department of Health and the Home Office appointed a committee under the chairmanship of Dr John Reed (Senior Principal Medical Officer, Department of Health) to review comprehensively the provisions of the health and social services in England by the NHS, Special Hospitals and local authorities for mentally disordered offenders (and others requiring similar services). The committee's remit extended to England only, but their work had implications for service provision in Scotland, Northern Ireland and Wales. At the conclusion of their work, in July 1992, the committee had produced several very detailed reports covering such matters as finance, staffing and training, research, academic development, and services for mentally disordered offenders with special needs (for example, learning disability). At a later stage, the committee also produced reports on psychopathic disorder and high security services.[8] Although not *specifically* concerned with the assessment of risk, the reports have important implications for risk assessment and management, particularly those dealing with resources, resource planning and staff training.

In their *Final summary report*, the committee point out some interesting historical facts relating to risk and risk assessment. They indicate that in the Middle Ages it was lawful to imprison someone if he or she was mentally disordered and people believed that he or she was going to commit some serious act like setting fire to a house. The committee went on to note how the Vagrancy Act of 1744 distinguished lunatics from 'rogues, vagabonds, sturdy beggars and vagrants' and also made provision for the apprehension of those who were 'furiously mad *and dangerous* . . . in such place . . . as the justices shall . . . direct and appoint' [emphasis added]. The committee also pointed out that the problems we are encountering today are not new. 'Almost 100 years ago, one Thomas Holmes described the "ever increasing army of the demented" coming before the magistrates' courts' (Department of Health & Home Office, 1992: 4).[9]

RECENT CONCERNS

In Chapter 1, I referred to public perceptions of danger as presented through the media. As a result of these perceived concerns, Government has, over the past few years, implemented various pieces of legislation that place risk, and public protection from it, as central guiding principles. This has been driven by a political philosophy, which Faulkner has cogently described in terms of 'exclusive' and 'inclusive' views of 'society and human relationships'. Faulkner (1998: 166–7) states that:

> The 'exclusive' view emphasises personal freedom and individual responsibility, but is inclined to disregard the influence of situations

and circumstances. It distinguishes between a deserving majority who are self-reliant, law-abiding and entitled to benefit themselves without interference from others; and an undeserving, feckless, welfare dependent and *often dangerous minority* or underclass from whom they need to be protected [emphasis added] . . . The contrasting 'inclusive' view recognises the capacity and will of individuals to change – to improve if they are given guidance, help and encouragement; to be damaged if they are abused or humiliated.

Current legislation seems to reflect the polarisation suggested by Faulkner. It is worth while examining some of this legislation in a little detail, as it reflects political perceptions of risk and its management.

The Criminal Justice Act 1991   Within this enactment a dangerous offender 'may be sentenced in the same manner as any other offender, in accordance with the "just deserts" philosophy expressed in Section 2(2)(a)' (Bolton, 1998: 3). However, under Section 2(2)(b) of the Act, where a court is satisfied that the offender presents a serious risk to the public and where the offender has committed a 'violent or sexual offence' the court may impose a longer than commensurate determinate sentence provided that this is not a greater sentence than the maximum sentence provided in law for that offence. The Act also provides for compulsory aftercare for such persons.[10] Under the Crime (Sentences) Act 1997, Crown Courts are *obliged* to impose long minimum sentences for serious crimes and, in some cases, may impose a mandatory life sentence for a second serious offence. This legislation has much in common with the 'three strikes and you're out' legislation in the United States. Public protection is also at the heart of further provisions in this Act to deal with psychopaths. Under Section 46 of the Act, two new Sections are introduced into the 1983 Mental Health Act (England and Wales). Crown Courts may impose a sentence of imprisonment, but attach what is known as a 'Hospital and Limitation Direction'. This is intended to enable a Crown Court to ensure that should the psychopathically disordered offender not respond to hospital treatment, he or she may be transferred to prison. There is provision in the Act for this mechanism to be applied to other types of mental disorder at some future date. Similar provisions apply in Scotland and in Northern Ireland. In Scotland, the Direction applies to all forms of mental illness; there is no separate category of psychopathic disorder in Scottish mental health legislation. The Northern Ireland legislation is similar to our own. The legislation, first proposed by the previous government, and somewhat to the surprise of many observers, put into effect by the present one, has not met with much approval. At the time of writing, no such orders seem to have been made by the courts (N. Shackleford, Home Office, personal communication, 27 August 1998). Similar strands of emphasis on public protection may be found in the Sex Offenders Act 1997. Part 1 of this Act requires offenders who commit certain sexual offences to inform the police where they are living and if they change their name or move. Failure to do so can entail imprisonment for up to six months or a fine of £5,000. *Depending on the degree of risk an individual may present*, the police are empowered in exceptional cases to pass details on to third parties [emphasis added]. The guidance offered in the Home Office Circular (39.1997) relating to the implementation of the Act, offers only fairly general guidance to the situations in which such information should be passed on; much appears to be left to the professional discretion of police officers, following consultation with other interested parties such as probation officers. Paragraph 34 of the circular merely states that 'Chief Officers are asked to ensure that officers and staff likely to be involved in this work in their force are aware of this guidance; and that there is a recognised framework for securing *rapid advice within the force to inform disclosure decisions*' [emphasis added]. Registration under the Act is subject neither to appeal nor review (except in the case of a successful appeal against conviction for the offences). The procedure applies to offenders who have been cautioned, were in custody or under supervision in the community as at 1 September 1997. It is applicable throughout the UK. Length of sentence will determine the length of registration. For example, a person imprisoned for thirty months or more will be on the register for life; a sentence between six months and thirty months will involve registration for ten years. The provisions have been given only a cautious response. The Association of Chief Officers of Probation (ACOP) have stated:

> It will be some time before the register becomes a comprehensive database and it will never contain the names of the many offenders who escape detection. It should not be perceived as an immediate panacea. The fanfares at its inception should not allow complacency towards building and maintaining the many other strands of activity that enhance public protection; from detection and conviction, all the way through to treatment and community supervision and surveillance.
>
> (As quoted in NACRO *Criminal Justice Digest:*
> *94*, October 1997: 1)

Soothill and Francis (1997: 1324–5) also have some cogent criticisms of the Act and what it may achieve. *First*, they suggest that one cannot regard sexual offenders as a 'homogenous group'. *Second*, since many sex offenders are at large for long periods before reconviction, there needs to be long-term follow-up to obtain a true picture of success. *Third*, sexual offenders *not* required to register under the Act appear to have similar rates of re-offending to those who *are* subject to the Act. 'Any assumption that the scheme "captures" the most active sexual offenders is untrue'. *Fourth*, Soothill and Francis suggest that there 'seems no criminological rationale to the determination of the periods of registration. The varying periods under different conditions seem to be more akin to continuing the punishment of sex offenders rather than representing appropriate measures to protect the public'. The authors conclude that the Act 'fails to identify [such offenders] in a systematic manner . . . In brief, the Act seems a political gesture which is probably misleading, potentially mischievous and almost certainly mistaken'.

The Crime and Disorder Act   Further power to regulate the behaviour of sex offenders is implemented in the Crime and Disorder Act which (as from 1 December 1998) introduces *Sex Offender Orders*. This will enable the police to apply to the courts for a civil order permitting the curtailment of the offender's freedom of activity (for example, placing further restrictions on certain forms of employment and prohibiting access to certain areas where children are likely to congregate etc.). The Minister of State at the Home Office, Alun Michael, stated that these orders 'will bring under supervision sex offenders who give cause for concern, regardless of the legislation under which they were originally sentenced. Severe penalties, including imprisonment, are available for those who fail to comply with the order' (letter to the *Independent*, 26 August 1998, p. 2). The first such order, in the form of a 'curfew', was made by a Manchester Magistrates' Court in December, 1998.

Bolton (1998) suggests that our legislation dealing with dangerous offenders is piecemeal. To a considerable extent this is true, and there are those who consider that it should be rationalised under one piece of legislation. She considers that we might learn from Canadian practice (Part XXIV of the Canadian Criminal Code). However, Slovenko (1998: 99) an American professor of Law and Psychiatry, suggests a degree of caution in espousing new provisions uncritically. Writing of recent American dangerous sexual psychopath legislation, he says:

As each new legal experiment is introduced, perhaps it would be to everyone's advantage if it were tested in the manner of a true experiment and information gathered about its effectiveness in enhancing community safety and fairness. From such an information base, in any country, the next legal steps might have more chance of achieving both.

In the UK at the present time, one has the feeling that such sensible suggestions would not find much favour with our political leaders. Recent and current legislation has all the hallmarks of piecemeal, idiosyncratic and knee-jerk responses to social problems, with little thought given to prior examination of outcomes. However, this legislation provides the current structures and frameworks under which professionals have to make judgements and decisions about risk. Some of these are now considered.

NATIONAL DECISION-MAKING AND ADVISORY BODIES[11]

The following three bodies are now considered: the Parole Board; the Mental Health Review Tribunal; and the Home Secretary's Advisory Board on Restricted Patients.

The Parole Board[12]

The arrangements for release on parole and life licence are contained in the Criminal Justice Acts of 1967, 1972 and 1991. The Act of 1967 established the Board as an independent body, appointed by the Home Secretary, to offer him or her advice and to take decisions on his or her behalf on the early release of determinate or life sentence prisoners. The Criminal Justice Act 1991 makes provision for all determinate sentence prisoners sentenced on or after 1 October 1992 and all life sentence prisoners, whenever they were sentenced, to be subject to the provisions of the Act. Unfortunately, there has proved to be a loophole in the Act as far as compulsory aftercare is concerned. As the media has not been loathe to point out, a very small group of notorious paedophiles have had to be released without the obligation of being placed under compulsory supervision, as they were sentenced before the 1991 Act came into force. As I write, yet another of these very small number of cases has hit the headlines. This concerns a man sentenced to ten years for very serious sexual assaults on children. He has allegedly refused treatment during his imprisonment; he has also refused to be placed voluntarily in secure accommodation. To make matters worse, he has decided to return to the small village where he committed some of his original offences. The police have established a helpline for the victims and offered help to worried parents living in the village. A leader in the *Independent* of 24 August 1998, p. 3 calls for such offenders to be kept in gaol, conveniently forgetting that once a person has completed a fixed sentence of imprisonment they have to be released. Until we give active consideration to special indeterminate sentences for such persons (assuming that a life sentence cannot be applied) the dilemma will remain. The same newspaper account states that the Prison Service is reviving its interest in the possibilities of chemical castration. However, as the same article points out 'The problem is in the mind not the genitals'. Calls for chemical castration usually omit to give serious consideration to the difficult ethical issues involved around questions of valid consent to such interventions. The available evidence also suggests that the use of anti-libidinal drugs on their own are usually ineffective, unless accompanied by some form of individual or group counselling.

The 1991 Act introduced two new schemes for the release of *determinate sentence* prisoners. The first is the *Automatic Conditional Release Scheme (ACR)* and applies to all prisoners serving less than four years. Such prisoners are released automatically at the half-way point in their sentence. The system is administered locally at the prisons where the offender is located. Prisoners serving sentences of *under twelve months* are released *unconditionally*. All young offenders and all adults serving twelve months and over are released on licence (issued on the Home Secretary's behalf by the Prison Governor). There is compulsory supervision from the date of release up to the three quarters point of sentence. Additionally, as was pointed out earlier, some sex offenders may be subject to supervision throughout the entire length of their sentence at the discretion of the sentencing judge. The second is the *Discretionary Parole Scheme*. The discretionary element in the previous parole system (1961 Act) is retained for prisoners serving four years and over. They become eligible for parole mid-sentence, but will be released automatically two thirds of the way through if parole is *not* granted. Parole Board members visit and interview the prisoner. The Board is responsible for the final decision on suitability for release of prisoners serving less than seven years and has to state reasons for its decision. For prisoners serving more than seven years, the Home Secretary retains final responsibility as to release, but is advised by the Board. All prisoners released under the discretionary scheme are under supervision and some sex offenders are supervised up to the end of sentence.

The Parole Board also deals with *life sentence* prisoners. They fall to be dealt with under two categories: Mandatory Life Sentence and Discretionary Life Sentence prisoners.

Mandatory Life Sentence prisoners (i.e. those given a life sentence for murder)   Three-member panels of the Board deal with these prisoners' cases. If the Board *does not* recommend release on licence, the Home Secretary *may not* sanction release. If the Board *does* recommend release, the Home Secretary *may* sanction release, but is not bound to do so. He is required to consult with the trial judge (if available) and the Lord Chief Justice in relation to tariff considerations.

Discretionary Life Sentence prisoners (i.e. those persons who have attracted a life sentence for crimes other than murder)   These cases are also dealt with by a three-member panel of the Board and take the form of oral hearings in prisons. Prisoners have a right to attend, to be legally represented and to call witnesses. Such a panel has the power to *direct* the Home Secretary to release the prisoner where the panel is satisfied that it is no longer necessary for the protection of the public for the prisoner to be detained.

Parole Board panels have to get to grips with three important elements. *First*, considerations relating to tariff. This is important if public confidence in the parole system is to be maintained, though it should not be the overriding consideration. *Second*, consideration needs to be given to the degree of progress that the prisoner has made during sentence in the eyes of the professionals concerned with his or her management. *Third*, the Board has an overriding concern with making judgements about public protection: 'Is it safe to release?' As I shall show in Chapter 5, such predictions are hazardous and depend for their success on adequate and accurate information being made available to the decision takers. In their annual *Report for 1996/7* the Board report on work being undertaken on improving risk assessment skills. A sample of parolees who failed on licence was being examined 'analysing both the parole and probation documents' . . . in an effort to identify 'ways the Parole Board and the probation service can improve risk assessment' (Parole Board for England and Wales, 1996/7: 9). At the time the *Report* was written, the results of the survey were not available.

Another development was for the provision of the judges' sentencing comments to be included in the parole files of those sentenced to imprisonment of four years and over. It was hoped that when they become routinely available they may serve as an aid to making an effective base-line in the risk assessment process. Judith Pitchers, a very experienced independent Parole Board member, refers to the Home Secretary's directions to the Board in relation to the determination of risk. She states (1995: 60) that the Board needs to be satisfied that:

1. Supervision is likely to reduce the likelihood of further re-offending. A small risk of violent re-offending is to be regarded as more serious than a larger risk of non-violent re-offending.
2. The prisoner has shown by his attitude and behaviour that he is willing to address his offending and has made efforts and progress in doing so.
3. The resettlement plan will assist rehabilitation.

The Home Secretary's directions to the Board place much emphasis on public protection. For example, in his directions concerning the release (and in some cases recall) of *determinate sentence* prisoners he states that:

> In deciding whether or not to recommend release on licence, the Parole Board shall consider *primarily* the risk to the public . . . and whether any such risk is acceptable. This must be balanced against the benefit, both to the public and to the offender, of early release back into the community under a degree of supervision which might help rehabilitation and so lessen the risk of re-offending in the future. The Board shall take into account that safeguarding the public may often outweigh the benefits of early release.
> (Parole Board for England and Wales, 1996/97, Appendix A: 41)

Concerning *mandatory life sentence* prisoners the Home Secretary has identified issues that may go beyond the risk posed by the prisoner if released: 'The Home Secretary is . . . concerned with the wider political implications, including the effect on public confidence in the life sentence system which release may have, i.e. how the public would be likely to respond to the lifer being released at that juncture' (Parole Board for England and Wales, 1996/97, Appendix B: 43).

The Home Secretary appears to be more specific concerning release in these cases than he is in respect of *determinate sentence* prisoners. For example:

The Parole Board's responsibilities in the release consideration are whether, having regard to the degree of risk involved of the lifer committing further imprisonable offences after release, it remains necessary for the protection of the public for the lifer to be confined.
(Parole Board for England and Wales, 1996/97, Appendix B: 43)

Such caution seems entirely offence–category related. For example, a person convicted of other homicide offences may present as much, or in some cases, more risk of re-offending than someone convicted of murder. Most observers now agree that the division between murder and other forms of homicide is arbitrary and many of the problems that arise in this area would be resolved if the mandatory life sentence was abolished.

THE MENTAL HEALTH REVIEW TRIBUNAL (MHRT)

Mental Health Review Tribunals were introduced by the Mental Health Act 1959.[13] They were intended to serve as a replacement for the role of the lay magistracy under previous lunacy legislation in safeguarding the rights of patients subject to detention; they also replaced some of the functions of the old Board of Control to which a patient could make representation against detention in hospital. The role and scope of the Tribunals were extended under the Mental Health Act 1983; the Act gives greater opportunities for appeal against detention and for automatic review of patients' cases at regular intervals if they have not applied themselves. The 1983 Act also gives wider powers to Tribunals to order the discharge of offender–patients detained under restriction orders. Under the 1959 Act, the Tribunal could only *recommend* discharge to the Home Secretary. The MHRT is a *judicial* body and, unlike the Parole Board, has considerable statutory powers which are independent of any government agency such as the Home Office. The main purpose of the MHRT is to review the cases of compulsorily detained patients and, if the relevant criteria are satisfied, to direct their discharge. This task involves examination of complex and often conflicting elements giving rise to concern for the liberty of the patient (or offender–patient) on the one hand, and the protection of the public on the other. There are MHRTs for each health authority region and the panels consist of three members: the legal member (who presides), the medical member (almost always a psychiatrist of considerable experience) and a so-called lay member, who is neither a lawyer nor a doctor. In hearing 'restricted' cases, the president is required to be a circuit judge or lawyer of equivalent status, such as a silk recorder. All three members have equal status, an equal role in the decision-making process and in drafting the reasons for the final decision. Hearings are almost always in private, but in certain circumstances, a patient may request a public hearing. These days, almost all patients are legally represented. In some particularly difficult or possibly contentious cases, other interested parties, such as the Home Office, may be legally represented, usually by counsel. Risk assessment will be a key consideration in all Tribunal hearings, but is likely to be most prominent in cases where an offender–patient has been made subject to a Hospital Order with restrictions (Sections 37/41 of the Act). Some aspects of the making of restriction orders, their effects and appeals against detention under them are now considered.[14]

Section 41 of the Mental Health Act 1983 enables a Crown Court to make a 'restriction order'. The criteria for making such an order are as follows:

1   That following conviction, it appears to the court, having regard to the

   (a)   nature of the offence
   (b)   the offender's antecedents and,
   (c)   the risk of his or her committing further offences if discharged, that a restriction order is necessary *for the protection of the public from serious harm.*

2   That at least one of the medical practitioners authorised under Section 12(2) of the Act whose written evidence is before the court has also given that evidence orally.

The criterion in italics did not appear in the 1959 Mental Health Act; it was inserted in the 1983 legislation to ensure that only those offender–patients who were considered likely to constitute a serious risk of harm to the public would be subject to the serious restrictions on liberty that follow the making of such an order (see below). Recent case law (*R.* v. *Courtney* (1987) and *R.* v. *Birch* (1989)) has made it clear that the risk of serious harm must be to the public *at large* and is not intended to apply when the harm (as for example in the case of homicide) has been directed in highly circumscribed circumstances to a *specific individual*, such as a spouse (see also Note 5 *supra*). A restriction order may be made either for a specific period or without time limit (the latter being the most frequently adopted course). The effects of a restriction order on those made subject to it are considerable:

1 The offender–patient cannot be given leave of absence from the hospital, be transferred elsewhere, or be discharged by the Responsible Medical Officer (RMO) without the consent of the Home Secretary.
2 The Home Secretary may remove the restrictions if he or she considers they are no longer required to protect the public from serious harm. Should the order remain in force without the restriction clause, it has the same effect as an order under Section 37 of the Act and any application for discharge from the order can be heard by an ordinary MHRT panel.

Applications for discharge from orders made under the civil powers of the Act are dealt with under Section 72; applications by restricted patients are considered under Section 42 and Sections 72 and 73 (taken together). Powers under these later sections are complicated to say the least, and their interpretation has been the subject of numerous High Court decisions taken under Judicial Review. During the years the 1959 Act was in force, hardly any cases went to such review. Since the inception of the 1983 Act, some forty-three cases have been dealt with by this means; the majority of them concerned with various aspects of discharge.[15] The availability of legal aid for Tribunal applicants and the problems of interpretation of the 1983 Act have almost certainly led to this considerable increase.

Under Section 73 of the Act a MHRT *must* order a restricted offender–patient's *absolute* discharge if it is satisfied that:

1 The offender–patient is not now suffering from one of the forms of mental disorder specified in the Act which makes it appropriate for him or her to be detained in hospital for medical treatment; *or*
2 It is not necessary for the health or safety of the offender–patient or for the protection of other persons that he or she should receive such treatment; *and*
3 It is not appropriate for the offender–patient to remain liable to be recalled to hospital for further treatment.

However, in the important case of *R.* v. *Kay* (1990), it was held by the court of appeal that a Tribunal which was satisfied that a restricted patient was not suffering from mental disorder was nevertheless entitled to order the conditional discharge of the offender–patient and was not, as had hitherto been held to be the case, obliged to order his or her absolute discharge. This decision would seem to be at odds with the intention of the 1983 Act since, taken together, Sections 72 and 73 appear to make it mandatory upon the Tribunal to discharge the patient absolutely in the absence of mental disorder. What the appeal court appeared to have in mind was the possibility of a need for a residual power to recall in the event of a relapse at some future date; the court held that this was an important discretionary power. Kay's case has now been decided upon by the European Court of Human Rights to the effect that evidence of a relapse in the patient's mental state (which may present a risk to others) is now the *only* legitimate reason for recall. This means that before a restricted patient can be recalled to hospital, there has to be *current* evidence of the existence of mental disorder [emphasis added]. Hitherto, this was not a requirement (*Kay* v. *United Kingdom* (1994)).

In the light of a Tribunal or the Home Secretary agreeing to an order for the conditional discharge of an offender–patient, the latter will be made subject to a number of conditions on release. These will almost always include supervision by a local authority social worker, or probation officer and a psychiatrist. Other requirements may include residence at a specified place and the avoidance of contact with specific individuals. The professionals supervising the offender–patient in the community are obliged to render progress reports to the Home Secretary at regular intervals. These reports will provide information as to general progress and, in cases where the offender–patient is causing particular concern, the professionals may recommend recall to hospital. It is in these cases that assessments of future risk to others are of crucial importance and aspects of this are dealt with in subsequent chapters. In the event of the Home Secretary ordering recall, the offender–patient's case must be referred to a MHRT within one month.[16]

Criticisms of MHRTs

In view of the fine balancing act that MHRTs have to perform, particularly in restricted cases, it is not entirely surprising that they have sometimes been criticised. Two recent homicide inquiries have highlighted some of these deficiencies. They are the inquiry into the case of Andrew Robinson (Blom-Cooper et al., 1995) and that into the case of Jason Mitchell (Blom-Cooper et al., 1996).

The case of Andrew Robinson

Whilst a detained in-patient at a psychiatric unit in Torbay, Andrew Robinson killed a young occupational therapist, Georgina Robinson (no relation). During his long history of psychiatric in- and out-patient care, Robinson had appeared before a number of Tribunals. At some of these, it is suggested that the details relating to his index offence (for which he had been made the subject of a Hospital Order with restrictions) and other aspects of his history, were deficient so that the Tribunals had to make decisions on inadequate evidence. There were suggestions that a significant feature of this inadequate base-line information was a down grading of his past behaviour and his potential to commit further serious harm. At one Tribunal, Robinson had refused to be examined by the medical member of the MHRT (a requirement under the Tribunal Rules). Despite this, the Tribunal went ahead and heard and determined the case, giving him an absolute discharge. Although the inquiry team made serious criticisms of the Tribunals' decision-making processes, it must be pointed out in fairness that the team also acknowledged that the Tribunals were acting on the information before them, and that this information was often seriously inadequate.

The case of Jason Mitchell

In the inquiry into the Mitchell case, the team (also led by Blom-Cooper) made more wide-ranging comments about what were, in their view, inadequacies in the MHRT system. In December 1994 Jason Mitchell, already subject to a restriction order, strangled two neighbours (who were unknown to him); some few days later he strangled his father and cut up his body. He had appeared before a MHRT in 1991; the Tribunal gave him a conditional discharge, but deferred it on grounds that the inquiry team deemed to be outside the Tribunal's powers. These were: (1) a reduction in medication; (2) a transfer to an open ward; and (3) unescorted leave outside the hospital. The purpose of a deferred conditional discharge is to enable the Tribunal to be satisfied that suitable arrangements for the applicant's management in the community can be made before the order is finally authorised by the Tribunal. Clearly the Tribunal which sat in 1991 was in error.

In 1993, Mitchell's case was referred to the MHRT by the Home Secretary (the earlier deferred conditional discharge not having been fulfilled). This time, a conditional discharge was implemented, the MHRT members acting on the assumption that they were merely endorsing the 1991 decision – a decision, as the inquiry team pointed out, which was legally flawed. Blom-Cooper and his colleagues made a number of recommendations, including the following: (a) Clinical forensic psychologists should be added to the list of 'lay' members who can be appointed to serve on MHRTs; (b) the MHRT should be in receipt of more detailed information concerning the offender–patient's index offence. (The Home Office (Mental Health Unit) has subsequently set in train procedures to give effect to this); (c) where the MHRT is dealing with a restricted case, the medical member of the Tribunal should be a forensic psychiatrist; (d) training for new and existing members of MHRTs should be improved. (Since the report (but not arising from it) more systematic training (Orientation) for recently appointed Tribunal members has been introduced. Plans are currently in hand to determine the needs of experienced members); and (e) MHRT members should be afforded follow-up; in cases where offender–patients re-offend in serious fashion after discharge, a confidential retrospective review should be held.[17]

The Home Secretary's Advisory Board on Restricted Patients

Following the conviction and sentence of the late Francis Graham Young for murder by poisoning, the Home Secretary, acting on the recommendation of the inquiry into Young's case (Home Office & DHSS, 1973), established a committee (known then as the Aarvold Board) to advise him in those restricted cases: (a) which were considered to be particularly problematic; (b) which were considered to need special care in assessment; and (c) where there was thought to be a fear of possible future risk to the public. This committee, now know as the Home Secretary's Advisory Board on Restricted Patients, merely proffers advice to the Home Secretary. It deals with only a very few cases; it is quite independent of the MHRT, and it would appear that its workload has decreased considerably in recent years. This leaves the MHRT as the sole body in cases where the Home Secretary has not approved the patient's conditional discharge himself. Membership of the Committee is small, and it includes a legal chairperson, psychiatrists, a director of social services, a chief probation officer and two other members who are considered to have wide experience of the criminal justice system. (See Egglestone, 1990, for a useful history of the Board and its functions).

CONCLUSION

It hardly needs stressing that the law and administrative practice concerning dangerous and potentially dangerous offenders are highly complex. The administrative systems for parole, life-licence and the conditional discharge of restricted patients have many common features. Recent developments in the administration of parole have much in common with MHRT procedure and practice (notably the offender's right to a personal hearing and to legal representation). However, the law seems to be scattered throughout a number of disparate enactments and there is something to be said for the view that a degree of rationalisation ought to be considered. Whatever the eventual outcome, the assessment of risk to the public is an overarching one. Subsequent chapters in this book examine the role of mental disturbance in the commission of serious violence; what lessons can be learned in relation to risk assessment in those cases where things appear to have gone wrong (notably in homicide cases); and in what ways we can try to improve our procedures and practices.

NOTES

1 See also Prins (1993); and see also Richardson (1993), Hoggett (1996), and Jones (1996). Stone (1995) provides a concise practical account of the law on mentally disordered offenders.

2 Sentencing issues more generally are dealt with comprehensively in Wasik (1998), and Sanders & Young (1997).

3 For the judgment in her case see *The Times* Law Report, 18 December 1997 p. 39: (QB Divisional Court) *R.* v. *Secretary of State for the Home Department, ex parte Hindley*. Currently, Hindley is said to be attempting to bring evidence to suggest that she was acting under the coercive influence of her co-accused Brady at the time of the murders.

4 Similar provisions are to be found in the legislation in Northern Ireland and Scotland. For a general review of 'dangerousness' in English law see Baker (1994).

5 For a discussion of the interpretation of 'serious harm' see Stone (1995: 71–2). See also Rix and Agarwal (1999).

6 Currently, the future of the three Special Hospitals is under active review. The disadvantages of large 'total' institutions have to be set against the advantages of specialist staffing within them and the problems likely to be encountered in re-locating some very highly dangerous patients in smaller units with less experienced staff. (See Fallon et al. 1999).

7 The history and use of the word 'danger' is of interest in the context of this chapter. Craft (1984) suggests that the first recorded use of the word occurred in 1523 and that its use in the civil and criminal courts gradually increased in the nineteenth century. The word certainly has very emotive connotations – hence, recent moves to replace it by the word 'risk'. The sociologist Nikolas Rose (1996) notes that we have recently seen a shift from the notion of dangerousness to that of risk. He suggests that this paradigm shift has important implications for all those engaged in the decision-making processes concerned with the management of those considered to be a danger to others. The thrust of responsibility seems to be shifting from 'dangerous individuals' to those responsible for managing them. Rennie (1978: 5) reminds us that 'for nearly four-hundred years, from the thirteenth through the sixteenth centuries, the English criminal law was obsessed with vagrants and beggars, who were viewed as a danger to society'. Foucault (1978) suggests that from the nineteenth century onwards, alienists (psychiatrists) were employed increasingly to delineate individuals as dangerous.

A glance in the direction of orthography and etymology is also helpful. Bowden (1985) suggests that the word 'danger' can be traced through the old French 'dangier' and the Anglo-French 'da(u)nger'. However, another derivation is also important for our purposes; namely, that provided by Sarbin (1967), who suggests that the word derives from the Latin 'dominarum', meaning 'lordship' or 'sovereignty'. He argues that this derivation has strong connotations of power relationships, and he considers this to be important because it is concerned with a person's concept of his [or her] social identity and the actions that he [or she] or others might take to confirm or deny this. (For a comprehensive review of the topic of dangerousness up to the middle 1970s, see Bottoms, 1977).

8 All seven reports repay careful examination. However, the *Final summary report* provides a very useful overview. (Department of Health & Home Office, 1992).

9 Some of these historical aspects have been ably (and indeed humorously) described by Allderidge (1979; 1985). Parker (1985: 15) has also contributed substantially to our knowledge in this area: 'The practice of confining some of the insane stretches back more than 600 years in England. The type of detained patient has varied, always including those considered to be dangerous . . . the forms of security employed have changed little over the period; perimeter security, internal locks and bars and individual restraint by both chemical and physical means have been in continuous use to a greater or lesser degree in various guises up to the present day.'

10 The concept of preventive incarceration is not new. The Prevention of Crimes Act 1908 provided for the detention of 'habitual criminals'; similar provisions were re-enacted in the Criminal Justice Act 1948 and in the 1961 Criminal Justice Act. These provisions were not *specifically* concerned with the 'dangerous' offender, but with 'habitual' criminals; they have since been repealed.

11 There are, of course, *local* advisory and decision-making bodies. For example, Area Criminal Justice Committees, *ad hoc* committees involved in risk taking, inquiries into 'serious incidents' such as homicide etc. Some of these are the subject of discussion in later chapters.

12 The Board must include amongst its members (Parole Board for England and Wales, 1996/7):

- A person who holds or has held judicial office.
- A psychiatrist.
- A person who has experience of the supervision or aftercare of discharged prisoners (usually a Chief Probation Officer).
- A person who has made a study of the causes of crime and the treatment of offenders (usually an academic criminologist).

The Board consists of a full-time chairperson, a part-time judicial chairperson, four full-time independent members (i.e. those not falling into any of the categories mentioned above) and over 60 part-time judicial, psychiatrist, probation, criminologist and independent members.

13 The MHRT is not to be confused with the Mental Health Act Commission. The Commission was established by the Mental Health Act 1983 to oversee the welfare and interests of detained patients. Some of its functions are to deal with complaints and to appoint 'second opinion doctors' who are required to intervene in certain circumstances when compulsory treatment is being proposed. It is also required to present a report on its work to Parliament every two years. It is important to note that the Commission has no power to order the release of detained patients; in this respect, it differs from the Mental Welfare Commission in Scotland (which has such powers in addition to its inspectorial functions). A detailed account of the functions of MHRTs in England and Wales may be found in *A Guide For Members* published by the Department of Health and updated at regular intervals (the latest edition 1996). For critical accounts of the current workings of the MHRT system, see Peay (1989) and Wood (1993).

14 An excellent guide to the *general* provisions of the 1983 Act may be found in *The maze*, (Bethlem and Maudsley, NHS Trust, 1997).

15 A detailed list of these decisions is to be found at Appendix VI of the *Guide for Members*, referred to in n13.

16 It is important to point out that there are certain other categories of restricted patients who have the right to apply to a Tribunal; these include those detained under the Criminal Procedure (Insanity and Unfitness to Plead) Act 1991, who have been found either unfit to plead or not guilty by reason of insanity. The other category of offender–patients concerns those who have been transferred from prison to hospital under Sections 47 and 48 of the 1983 Act. Only an outline account of the powers and procedures for the discharge of restricted patients is given in this chapter. Readers are strongly advised to consult Jones (1996), especially at pp. 251–66. For information about tribunal procedure see Gostin and Fennell (1992).

17 A useful summary of the inquiry team's findings in this case may be found in Brunning (1996); I have drawn heavily on Dr Brunning's account in presenting my own.

REFERENCES

Legal cases cited

R. v. Birch [1989] Court of Appeal. *Independent* Law Reports, 12 May: 14.

R. v. Courtney [1987] Court of Appeal. *Crim. Law Rev*, February 1988: 130.

R. v. Secretary of State for the Home Department ex parte Hindley [1997] *The Times* Law Reports, 19 December: 39.

R. v. Merseyside Mental Health Review Tribunal ex parte K. [1990] 1 All ER 694, CA.

R. v. Secretary of State for the Home Department ex parte K. [1990] 1 All ER 703.

Kay v. *United Kingdom* [1994] Report of the ECHR.

Text references

Allderidge, P. (1979). Hospitals, madhouses and asylums: Cycles in the care of the insane. *British Journal of Psychiatry*, *134*, 321–4.

Allderidge, P. (1985). Bedlam, fact or phantasy? In W.F. Bynum, R. Porter & M. Shepherd (eds), *The anatomy of madness: Essays in the history of psychiatry: Vol. 2 Institutions and Society*. London: Tavistock.

Baker, E. (1994). Dangerousness in English law. *International Bulletin of Law and Mental Health*, *5*, 40–2.

Bethlem and Maudsley NHS Trust. (1997). *The maze: Mental Health Act 1983: Guidelines*, London: Mental Health Act Department, Maudsley Hospital.

Blom-Cooper, L., QC, Hally, H., & Murphy, E. (1995). *The falling shadow: One patient's mental health care: 1978–1993*, London: Duckworth.

Blom-Cooper, L., QC, Grounds, A., Guinan, P., Parker A., & Taylor, M. (1996). *The case of Jason Mitchell: Report of the independent panel of inquiry*. London: Duckworth.

Bolton, L. (1998). Dangerous liaisons: Violent offenders and the law. *Forensic Up-Date*, *52*, 3–8.

Bottoms, A.E. (1977). Reflections on the renaissance of dangerousness. *Howard Journal of Penology and Crime Prevention*, *16*, 70–96.

Bowden, P. (1985). Psychiatry and dangerousness: A counter renaissance. In L. Gostin (ed.), *Secure provision: A review of Social Services for the mentally ill and mentally handicapped in England and Wales*. London: Tavistock.

Brunning, J. (1996). The case of James Mitchell: Report of the independent panel of inquiry. *Mental Health Review Tribunal Members' Newsheet*, *17*, 5–7.

Craft, M. (1984). Predicting dangerousness and future convictions among the mentally abnormal. In M. Craft and A. Craft (eds), *Mentally abnormal offenders*. London: Baillière Tindall.

Department of Health, & Home Office. (1992). *Review of health and social services for mentally disordered offenders and others requiring similar services: Final summary report*. Cmnd 2088. (Chairman Dr John Reed, CB). London: HMSO.

Egglestone, F. (1990). The Advisory Board on restricted patients. In R. Bluglass & P. Bowden (eds), *Principles and practice of forensic psychiatry*. London: Churchill Livingstone.

Fallon, P., QC, Bluglass, R., Edwards, B., & Daniels, G. (1999). *Report of the committee of inquiry into the personality disorder unit, Ashworth Special Hospital*. Cmnd 4194(1) and (2). Plus executive summary. London: HMSO.

Faulkner, D. (1998). Building a system on evidence and principle: Law structure and practice. *Vista, 3*, 164–80.

Floud J., & Young W. (1981). *Dangerousness and criminal justice*. London: Heinemann.

Foucault, M. (1978). About the concept of the 'dangerous individual' in 19th century legal psychiatry. *International Journal of Law and Psychiatry, 1*, 1–18.

Gostin, L., & Fennell, P. (1992). *Mental health: Tribunal procedure* (2nd ed.). London: Longman.

Hoggett, B. (Hon. Mrs Justice Hale). (1996). *Mental health law* (4th ed.). London: Sweet and Maxwell.

Home Office, & Department of Health and Social Security. (1973). *Report on the review of procedures for the discharge and supervision of psychiatric patients subject to special restrictions* (Aarvold Report, Cmnd 5191). London: HMSO.

Home Office and Department of Health and Social Security (DHSS). (1975). *Report of the committee on mentally abnormal offenders* (Chairman, Lord Butler of Saffron Walden, Cmnd 6244). London: HMSO.

Home Office. (1995). *Dealing with dangerous people: The probation service and public protection*. London: Home Office.

Inch, H., Rowlands, P., & Soliman, A. (1995). Deliberate self-harm in a young offenders' institution. *Journal of Forensic Psychiatry, 6*, 161–71.

Jones R. (1996). *Mental Health Act manual* (5th ed.). London: Sweet and Maxwell.

Little, M., & Gibbons, J. (1993). Predicting the rate of children on the child protection register. *Research Policy and Planning, 10*, 15–18.

National Association for the Care and Resettlement of Offenders. (1997). *Criminal Justice Digest* 94. London.

Parker, E. (1985). The development of secure provision. In L. Gostin (ed.), *Secure provision: A review of special services for the mentally ill and mentally handicapped in England and Wales*. London: Tavistock.

Parole Board for England and Wales. (1996/7). *Report for 1996/7* 252. London: HMSO.

Peay, J. (1989). *Tribunals on trial: A study of decision making under the Mental Health Act, 1983*. Oxford: Clarendon Press.

Pitchers, J. (1995). Parole and risk assessment. In J. Braggins & C. Martin (eds), *Managing risk: Achieving the possible*. London: Institute for the Study and Treatment of Delinquency.

Prins, H. (1993). Service provision and facilities for the mentally disordered offender. In K. Howells & C.R. Hollin (eds), *Clinical approaches to the mentally disordered offender*. Chichester: Wiley.

Prins, H. (1995a). *Offenders, deviants or patients?* (2nd ed.). London: Routledge.

Prins, H. (1995b). 'I've got a little list' (Koko: *Mikado*), but is it any use? Comments on the forensic aspects of supervision registers for the mentally ill. *Medicine, Science and the Law, 35*, 218–24.

Rennie, Y. (1978). *The search for criminal man*. Toronto: Laxington.

Richardson, G. (1993). *Law, process and custody: Prisoners and patients*. London: Weidenfeld and Nicolson.

Rix, K., & Agarwal, M. (1999). Risk of serious harm or a serious risk of harm? A trap for judges. *Journal of Forensic Psychiatry, 10*, 187–96.

Rose, N. (1996). Psychiatry as a political science: Advanced liberalism and the administration of risk. *History of Human Sciences, 9*, 1–23.

Sanders, A., & Young, R. (1997). *Criminal justice*. London: Butterworth.

Sarbin, T.R. (1967). The dangerous individual: An outcome of social identity transformations. *British Journal of Criminology, 7*, 285–95.

Scottish Council on Crime. (1975). *Crime and the prevention of crime*. London: HMSO.

Shaw, R. (1991). Supervising the dangerous offender: Communication the vital but often missing factor. *NASPO News, 10*, 3–12.

Slovenko, R. (1998). Sex offender legislation. *Criminal Behaviour and Mental Health, 8*, 95–99.

Soothill, K., & Francis, B. (1997, 5 September and 12 September). Sexual reconvictions and the Sex Offenders Act, 1997. *New Law Journal*, 1285–6 and 1324–5.

Stone, N. (1995). *A companion guide to mentally disordered offenders*. Ilkley: Owen Wells.

Wasik, M. (1998). *Emmins on sentencing* (3rd ed.). London: Blackstone Press.

Wood, Sir John. (1993). Reform of the Mental Health Act 1983: An effective tribunal system. *British Journal of Psychiatry, 162*, 14–22.

Chapter 3

Serious mental disturbance and violence

It is the very error of the moon;
She comes more near the earth than she was wont,
And makes men mad.

Othello, V, ii

In the context of this book, it would not be an exaggeration to describe views concerning the relationship between mental disturbance and crime as something of a battlefield; in addition, the myths reflected in Othello's words have also played their part. This chapter deals with the following aspects: definitions; general comments on mental disturbance and crime; serious mental disturbance and violence; and the prevalence of mental disturbances in various populations. The problems relating to female offenders are not addressed specifically in this chapter, solely because males tend to predominate in the exercise of violent acts.[1] For the purpose of this chapter, violence is used to denote serious crimes against persons or property (for example, homicide, serious assaults (sexual and otherwise), kidnapping and arson).

The term 'mental disturbance' is used here to include mental disorder as defined in the Mental Health Act 1983 in England and Wales. This includes mental illness (which in the Act is not further defined), mental impairment, severe mental impairment, psychopathic disorder and any other disorder or disability of mind.[2] The use of the term 'mental disturbance' also enables us to consider a wide range of other disorders and abnormalities, some of which – for example, severe personality disorder – would not satisfy the somewhat strict criteria for compulsory admission under the Mental Health Act. Admittedly, 'mental disturbance' is a somewhat vague term and, as we have seen, it has certainly led to difficulties for the courts in trying to determine what constitutes such an abnormality within the meaning of the Homicide Act 1957. NACRO's Mental Health Advisory Committee, in a series of Policy Papers, produced the following definition (NACRO, 1993: 4) of mental disturbance which encapsulates some of the problems referred to above:

> The term 'mentally disturbed offender' is defined here as:- those offenders who may be acutely or chronically mentally ill; those with neuroses, behavioural and/or personality disorders; those with learning difficulties; some who, as a function of alcohol and/or substance misuse, have a mental health problem; and any who are suspected of falling into one or other of these groups. It also includes those offenders where a degree of mental disturbance is recognised even though that may not be severe enough to bring it within the criteria laid down by the Mental Health Act 1983. It also applies to those offenders who, even though they do not fall easily within this definition – for example some sex offenders and some abnormally aggressive offenders – may benefit from psychological treatments.[3]

It is, in many ways, comparatively easy to define mental illnesses, especially those with clear-cut aetiology; it is somewhat less easy to define with any degree of acceptable precision such conditions as learning disability, particularly in its milder manifestations and, as we shall see, conditions such as personality (psychopathic) disorder. However, what we do know with some certainty is that mental disturbance is present in all walks of life including, most worryingly, that of our political and other leaders. From time to time this has had (and continues to have) frightening consequences (see, for example, Freeman, 1991).

SWITCHING GOALPOSTS

It is very difficult in many cases to establish clear causal connections, or even associations, between mental disturbance and criminality. This is because we are trying to make connections between very different phenomena, and these phenomena are the subject of much debate concerning both substance and definition. It is as though the goalposts for the game are constantly being switched. Let us take mental disturbance first. There are those who seek to suggest that some forms of mental disturbance do not even exist. A major proponent of this view is that redoubtable critic of psychiatry and psychiatrists, Professor Szasz, himself a psychoanalytic psychiatrist. In one of his books (Szasz, 1987) he summaries most of what he has said on this topic over several decades; namely, that persons are often diagnosed as mentally disturbed on the grounds that they have problems in living and that these problems affront society, and that therefore psychiatry is used to remove them from public view and conscience. This is a very bald and somewhat over-simplified view of Szasz's work. His arguments have an attractive seductiveness but they also contain elements of rhetoric, which have been criticised cogently by other psychiatrists and non-psychiatrists.

In the 1960s there existed a popular view that much mental illness had its origins in 'conspiracies' and 'mixed messages' within families. At the other end of the spectrum we have the more biological–psychiatric view as set out, for example, in some standard textbooks of psychiatry. Professor Gunn (1977: 317) put the position into perspective very well, when he stated:

> Somewhere in the confusion there is a biological reality of mental disorder . . . this reality is a complex mixture of diverse conditions, some organic, some functional, some inherited, some learned, some acquired, some curable, others unremitting.

This complex picture is also compounded by the fact that the prevalence and presentation of mental disturbance appears to change over time. Hard facts concerning the epidemiology and substance of such disorders, even for periods as recent as the nineteenth century, are not easy to come by. Some researchers have concluded, albeit tentatively, that the schizophrenic illnesses as we know them today possibly did not exist on any large scale in earlier times. However, anecdotal and some clinical evidence would indicate that this assertion needs to be viewed with some caution.

It is also worth mentioning that in earlier times there may well have been individuals presenting with psychiatric symptoms in whom, these days, we would recognise a physical or organic origin. In the middle ages, for example, malnutrition produced pellagric states with their psychological and psychiatric consequences. The use of bad flour probably produced ergot poisoning which in turn could produce signs and symptoms of psychiatric illness. It has been suggested that episodes of the 'dancing mania' seen in mediaeval Italy and neighbouring countries were due to such a cause. Lead was commonly used in making cooking utensils and for water pipes; this could produce lead poisoning which in turn could produce confused and disturbed behaviour.

Occupations also have their hazards. Few people can recall why Lewis Carroll described the Hatter at the tea party as 'mad'; he did so because people who worked in the hat-making industry might be exposed to mercury, and mercurial poisoning can produce signs and symptoms of so-called mental illness. It has been suggested that Isaac Newton's well-known episodes of withdrawal from public life and activity may have been due not to depressive illness, as had been thought hitherto, but to the effects of mercuric substances with which he experimented. It is of some interest to note that we are currently concerned about the effects of lead emissions, particularly on children's behaviour; and there are those who believe that poor-quality diet (particularly if it includes large quantities of junk foods and additives) can produce hyperactive and anti-social behaviour in some children. However, firm evidence of this, both in the USA and in Britain is hard to come by.

When we come to consider criminal behaviour we are faced with problems similar to those outlined above. At its simplest, crime is merely that form of behaviour defined as illegal and punishable by the criminal law. At various times in our history, acts judged as criminal have been redefined, or even removed from the statute books – as, for example, in the case of attempted suicide and adult male consenting homosexual acts committed in private. As we saw in Chapter 2, *new* offences are also created, most notably in times of war, civil commotion, or as a result of 'moral panics'. Moreover, our increasingly complex technological society has necessitated the introduction of a wide range of regulations governing many aspects of our conduct. Since much criminal behaviour is somewhat arbitrarily defined, and there are arguments about the existence and definition of mental abnormalities (disturbance), it is hardly surprising that we experience difficulty in trying to establish connections between these two somewhat ill-defined and complex behaviours. In view of this, it is even less surprising that we find difficulties in estimating the number of mentally disordered offenders in penal and other populations (see later). Whatever the difficulties may be, there are a number of occasions when mental disturbances seem to be closely associated with criminal conduct and some aspects of this connection are now considered in more detail.

AN OUTLINE CLASSIFICATION OF MENTAL DISORDERS (DISTURBANCES)

Some readers may wish to remind themselves of the manner in which the main mental disorders (disturbances) are commonly classified. It should be noted that this is a very rough and ready classification. Readers

Table 3.1 Outline classification of mental disorders (disturbances)

The functional psychoses	the affective disorders schizophrenic illnesses
The neuroses (psychoneuroses, neurotic reactions)	mild depression anxiety states hysteria (hysterical reactions) obsessional states
Mental disorder as a result of infection, disease, metabolic and similar disturbances, trauma	including the epilepsies[a]
Mental disorder due to the ageing process Abnormality of personality (psychopathic disorder) and sexual disorders	for example, the dementias
Substance abuse (alcohol, other drugs, solvents, etc.)	
Mental impairment (learning disability); also known as mental handicap, retardation[b]	including chromosomal abnormalities

Source: Modified from Prins (1995: 90).[c]

Notes

a Strictly speaking, the epilepsies are not mental disorders as such but are *neurological* disturbances (disorders). They are included here because they sometimes produce psychological and psychiatric disturbances.

b This condition has been known throughout history by many different names. Fortunately, some of the older and more pejorative terms, such as feeble-mindedness, idiocy, deficiency, amentia, are now no longer used.

c The somewhat arbitrary nature of the above classification is fairly obvious. It is also important to recognise that many of these disorders will overlap and that their prevalence may appear to change over time and be much influenced by social norms. This is of great importance at the present time because of justified concerns about possible misdiagnoses of mental disturbances in certain ethnic minority groups such as African-Caribbeans. The classification is offered merely to provide a context for the discussion.

wishing to pursue this aspect should consult *DSM – IV*, American Psychiatric Association (1994) and *ICD – 10*, World Health Organisation (1992) and any recent standard text-book of psychiatry, such as *The Oxford Text Book of Psychiatry* or *The Companion to Psychiatric Studies*.

As already mentioned, the problems of establishing relationships between mental disturbances and crime and, in particular, violent crime, are very considerable. Older studies show enormous disparities as to prevalence. Some twenty years ago, in the first edition of *Offenders, deviants or patients?* I attempted to demonstrate some of the disparities revealed in studies that had been carried out over a fifty- to sixty-year period (Prins, 1980). To facilitate ease of assimilation I classified the information by nature of disorder and tried to indicate the size of the sample surveyed (where such information was available). The samples were drawn mainly from penal and court clinic populations. As I shall demonstrate shortly, recent studies have used more highly developed statistical techniques with more reliable and less incongruous results. Despite the imperfections of these early studies, they are worth noting and are therefore displayed in Table 3.2.

MORE RECENT EPIDEMIOLOGICAL STUDIES

A short account is now given of some more recent epidemiological studies. In the UK:

> Although the actual number of prisoners requiring psychiatric services is not known, research has shown that the prison population has a high psychiatric morbidity . . . It is estimated that 2–3 per cent of *sentenced* prisoners at any one time are likely to be suffering from a psychotic illness, and it is likely that the proportion is even higher in the remand population. Histories of alcohol and drug misuse are very common, as is neurotic illness.
> (Home Office & Department of Health, 1991: Annex C)

The above extract provides an overall picture; some more detailed studies of both penal and hospital populations are now considered.

Penal populations

It would appear, from a variety of studies, that about one third of the prison population requires some kind of psychiatric intervention and that in remand populations this number increases. (For a summary of some of this research see Prins, 1995: 46–9.) Gunn et al. (1991a; 1991b) examined a series of sentenced prisoners in England and Wales. They contended, by extrapolation from their sample, that 'The sentenced population include[d] over 700 men with psychosis, and around 1,100 would warrant transfer to hospital for psychiatric treatment (1991a: 338). Since that survey was carried out, the prison population has increased to a considerable degree, so it would be reasonable to estimate that the disordered population would currently be even higher.

Two more recent and somewhat worrying studies add to the above picture. Birmingham et al. (1996) examined 569 men aged 21 years

Table 3.2 Prevalence of psychiatric disorders in penal populations

Nature of disorder	Percentage	Size of population	Author(s) of study and date
Psychosis (schizophrenia, affective disorders)	12%	608	Glueck (1918)
	0.6%	1,380	Thompson (1937)
	26%	100	Oltman & Friedman (1941)
	1.5%	10,000	Bromberg & Thompson (1947)
	1.5%	66 (homicides)	Gillies (1965)
	12%	50 (homicides)	Tupin, Mahar, & Smith (1973)
	10%	100	West (1963)
	0.5%	149 (Approved School boys)	Scott (1964)
	2%	300	Bluglass (1966)
	10%	289	Guze (1976)
	3%	75	Faulk (1976)
Mental subnormality (learning disability)[a]	28%	608	Glueck (1918)
	2.6%	1,380	Thompson (1937)
	16%	100	Oltman & Friedman (1941)
	2.4%	10,000	Bromberg & Thompson (1947)
	2.4%	91	Woddis (1964)
	14%	300	Bluglass (1966)
	6%	not given	Gibbens (1966)
Psychopathy (sociopathy)	19%	609	Glueck (1918)
	5.6%	1,380	Thompson (1937)
	14%	100	Oltman & Friedman (1941)
	6.9%	10,000	Bromberg & Thompson (1947)
	60%[b]	149 (Approved School boys)	Scott (1964)
	27%	66 (homicides)	Gillies (1965)
	13%	300	Bluglass (1966)
	70%	289	Guze (1976)
Psycho-neurosis (neurosis)	3.0%	100	Oltman & Friedman (1941)
	6.9%	10,000	Bromberg & Thompson (1947)
	7.9%	304 (boys in detention centre)	Banks (1964)
	2.0%	300	Bluglass (1966)

Table 3.2 (cont'd)

Nature of disorder	Percentage	Size of population	Author(s) of study and date
Alcoholism/ excess/heavy drinking	51%	500 (traffic offenders)	Selling (1940)
	50%	not given	Banay (1942)
	80%	not given	Cramer & Blacker (1963)
	55%	66 (homicides)	Gillies (1965)
	56%	50 (discharged male offenders)	Maule & Cooper (1996)
	11%	300	Bluglass (1966)
	40%	404	Gibbens & Silberman (1970)
	37%	90	Gunn (1973)

Source: Modified from Prins (1980).[c]

Notes

a For reasons of space the relationship between learning disability and violence is not considered in this chapter. To pursue this topic, see Prins (1995: 109–13) and Day (1993; 1997: 280–91).

b Personality disorder.

c For expansion on the sources and figures provided in Table 3.2 see Chapter 3 in Prins (1980), and Chapter 4 in Prins (1995).

and over *on remand waiting trial.* Of these, 26 per cent had one or more current mental disorders (excluding substance misuse), including 24 men who were acutely psychotic. A total of 168 men required psychiatric treatment, 50 of whom required urgent intervention; 16 required immediate transfer to psychiatric hospitals (see also Birmingham et al., 1998).

Brooke et al. (1996) examined 750 prisoners representing a 9.4 per cent cross-sectional sample of males in an *unconvicted* prison population. They diagnosed 63 per cent of inmates as having a psychiatric disorder. Main diagnoses in their survey were: substance misuse, 38 per cent; neurotic illness, 26 per cent; personality disorder, 11 per cent; psychosis, 5 per cent. The level of psychosis was calculated to be four to five times the level found in the general population. In 1985, Taylor reported on 303 male remanded prisoners, gathering data on current offence, mental state and socio-psychiatric history. This study showed (Taylor, 1985: 491; see also Taylor & Gunn, 1984) that all but 9 of a sub-group of 121 psychotic men:

showed active symptoms at the time of committing a criminal offence; 20% of the actively ill psychotics were driven directly to offend by their psychotic symptoms, and a further 26% probably so . . . within the psychotic group, those driven by their delusions were most likely to have been seriously violent and psychotic symptoms probably accounted directly for most of the very violent behaviour.

Studies of hospital and community populations

The vexed nature of the relationship between mental disturbances and criminality is illustrated when one examines the somewhat conflicting findings in various psychiatric patient studies. Modestin and Ammann (1995) studied an unselected sample of 1,265 in-patients and a matched control group drawn from the general population. Detailed accounts of conviction records served as a measure of criminal behaviour. They found (p. 667) that alcoholism and drug abuse contributed significantly to criminal behaviour 'independent of socio-demographic factors; however, with a few exceptions mental disorders such as schizophrenia and affective disorders do not contribute to criminal behaviour'. A somewhat different perspective is afforded in a significant study by Humphreys et al. (1994). They reported on offending among *first episode* schizophrenics. They found that 16 per cent of a large group of individuals in their first episode of schizophrenia had committed an offence within a five-year period *immediately prior to the initial admission to hospital* [emphasis added]. Of 55 recorded offences, most were minor. However, about half of the patients were 'clearly ill at the time of the offence, and a significant proportion were acting in direct response to psychotic symptoms' (p. 51).

Belfrage (1998) examined 1,056 mental patients with a diagnosis of 'schizophrenia, affective psychosis and paranoia' who were discharged from mental hospitals in Stockholm in 1986 and followed up ten years later. He found a major over-representation of criminality among the sample. Of those who were 40 years old or younger at the time of discharge, nearly 40 per cent had a criminal record (as compared to less than 10 per cent of the general public). The most frequently occurring crimes were of violence. Belfrage concludes that for various methodological reasons, the figures quoted are likely to be minimum figures.

In a very recently reported survey, Bland et al. (1998) conducted a study of a random sample of 3258 community residents in Edmonton,

Canada and 180 male prisoners below the age of 45; these latter were compared with males from the larger community sample in the same age group (n=924). The prisoner sample consisted of those who received prison sentences of less than two years. They report that 90 per cent of their sample had some form of psychiatric disorder at some time in their lives and 87 per cent had abused alcohol and other drugs. Over 76 per cent had shown some kind of symptomatology in the preceding six months. The researchers found higher prevalence rates for most psychiatric disorders than those in the community sample. This was most marked for substance abuse and personality disorders. In commenting on the implications of their findings they state (Bland et al., 1998: 278):

> The present system of numerous brief sentences, for often minor offences by a population that is socially and psychiatrically disadvantaged . . . [where] little or no treatment or rehabilitation is given, appears to serve no one very well.

Further light is thrown on the problem in another recently reported survey – this time from Australia. Wallace et al. (1998) examined those convicted in the higher courts in Victoria, Australia between 1993 and 1995, exploring their psychiatric histories by 'case linkage' to a register listing virtually all contacts with the public psychiatric services. They found prior psychiatric contact in 25 per cent of offences; personality disorder and substance abuse accounted for much of this relationship; schizophrenia and affective disorders were also over-represented, *particularly those with co-existing substance misuse* [emphasis added]. However, they conclude their survey with a note of caution: 'increased risk of offending by those suffering from functional psychosis is small and does not justify subjecting them, as a group, to either institutional containment or greater coercion' (p. 477). By definition, Special Hospital populations will show high rates of serious mental disorder, notably functional psychosis, learning disability and severe personality disorder. Taylor et al. (1998) surveyed the records of 1,740 Special Hospital patients resident at any time between 1 January and 30 June 1993. The survey, which was methodologically very sophisticated, included access to official criminal records. They found that 58 per cent had functional psychoses, 26 per cent had personality disorders and 16 per cent had learning disabilities. Fewer than 10 per cent had never been convicted of a criminal offence.[4] Direct personal violence was more common in men and fire-raising in women. Schizophrenia was most strongly associated with personal violence and more than 75 per cent of those with psychosis were recorded as being driven by their delusions (p. 172).

SCHIZOPHRENIC ILLNESS, AFFECTIVE DISORDER, PERSONALITY DISORDER AND VIOLENCE

Apart from severe personality disorder, schizophrenic illnesses seem to have the strongest relationship to the commission of serious personal violence.

Schizophrenic illnesses

It is best to consider the term schizophrenia as covering a group of illnesses rather than a single illness entity (see Prins, 1995). Evidence from a range of studies over the past two decades suggests a real, if very small, relationship between violence and schizophrenic illness (and in particular, paranoid type illness; see later). Evidence for such a relationship may be found in Gunn (1992), McNeil et al. (1998), Swanson et al. (1990), Lindquist and Allebeck (1990), Hodgins (1992), Wesseley et al. (1994), Monahan (1992), Taylor (1995), Link et al. (1992), and Link and Stueve (1994). Active delusions seem to be powerful factors in relation to violence where the patient perceives some threat, where there is a lessening of mechanisms of self-control and dominance of the patient's mind by perceived forces that seem to be beyond his or her control. (These are sometimes described in the literature as threat/control–override symptoms.)

Hodgins (1995: 5) makes some important observations on the relationship between major mental disorders and criminality. She states:

> Three lines of evidence indicate that persons who suffer from major mental disorders . . . [schizophrenia and major affective disorder] . . . are at increased risk, as compared to non-disordered persons, to commit crimes repetitively. This evidence suggests that the differences between the mentally disordered and the non-disordered populations are even greater for violent and non-violent criminality.

The three lines of evidence that she refers to come from international studies of unselected birth cohorts; from follow-up studies of psychiatric patients released into the community; and from surveys of mental disorder among convicted offenders (see earlier discussion). Hodgins describes two types of offender with major mental disorders: (1) 'early starters' who show a stable pattern of anti-social behaviour from an early age and (2) 'late starters' who begin only at about the time the 'symptoms of the major disorder become apparent' (p. 5). Hodgins suggests that major disorder is not related to the criminality of the 'early starters'; on the other hand, the symptoms of the disorder may be related closely to the delinquency of the 'late starters'.

Reference was made earlier in this chapter to the role of substance misuse in relation to major mental illnesses. Wheatley (1998: 14) studied a sample of schizophrenic patients in an independent health sector medium secure unit, detained under the Mental Health Act 1983. His results confirmed a high degree of co-morbidity of substance abuse and schizophrenia in detained and forensic patients. Alcohol and cannabis featured prominently; opiate use was rare. The author concludes that substance use and misuse are significant factors in risk assessment (see also Marshall, 1998).

In a large-scale and continuing American study, Steadman and his colleagues (1998) found in patients discharged from psychiatric hospitals that the incidence of violence was substantially elevated by the abuse of drugs and alcohol, when compared with others in the same neighbourhoods.

Paranoid disorders and dangerous obsessions

> Were my wife's liver
> Infected as her life, she would not live
> The running of one glass.
> Leontes in *The Winter's Tale*, I, ii

One of the key characteristics of those suffering from one or other of the various forms of paranoid illness is their systematised delusional belief (and sometimes hallucinatory experience). This may take the form of an irrational and unshakeable belief that they are being persecuted by others or, that they have a need to be the persecutor. (It is important to note that such systems of belief are not peculiar to those suffering from a schizophrenic disorder; they may be part of an affective illness or be associated with chronic alcohol abuse or, in some cases, organic disorder.) The finer points of classification need not concern us here; those wishing to explore these further should consult one or other of the text-books already referred to. Notorious cases do not need detailed recapitulation here (for example, Ian Ball's kidnap attempt on Princess Anne in London's Mall, Hinckley's attempt to assassinate President Reagan, and the delusional system developed by Peter Sutcliffe leading him to the serial killing of prostitutes and those he thought were prostitutes). There are two points of cardinal importance that should be noted by professionals who have to deal with such people. *First*, they may begin to develop certain oddnesses of behaviour for some time *before the disorder emerges in an acute or very obvious form*; sensitive observation and possible intervention *may*, in some cases, help to prevent a tragedy. However, it has to be realistically acknowledged that this may be very difficult on both clinical and ethical grounds. *Second*, persons developing paranoid beliefs may do so in an encapsulated (contained) form; thus a seriously paranoid person is highly likely to appear perfectly sane and in command of him- or herself in all other respects. The illness may be so well encapsulated that an unwary or unskilled observer may be very easily misled. It is only when the matters which the delusional system has fastened on are broached, that the severity of the disorder is revealed.

The sinister and potentially highly dangerous nature of these forms of disorder are clearly demonstrated in the condition variously described as 'morbid jealousy', 'sexual jealousy', 'delusions of infidelity' etc. For this reason I propose to deal with these conditions in some detail, since they are capable of extrapolation to other behaviours where obsessional ideas become potentially very dangerous. Another reason for including them here is that the apparently fairly recent phenomenon of stalking has led forensic psychiatrists and criminal justice professionals to take an increasing interest in a whole range of individuals who seem to show dangerous or potentially dangerous obsessive ideas about others. Some of the professional literature in this area tends to deal with these states of mind in discrete categories – for example, 'delusional jealousy', certain other paranoid conditions and a variety of presentations that generally go under the rubric of 'erotomania'. I suggest that it might be more useful to abandon these discrete categories and consider the totality of these phenomena within a framework of 'dangerous obsessions', irrespective of the focus of the unwanted attentions. I recognise that I am dealing here with very selective aspects of dangerous obsessions; others are equally dangerous, particularly when they are motivated by overwhelming desires for control and subjugation (see discussion of psychopathic disorder).

Many years ago, Lagache (1947) made the important observation that love involved two elements: a desire to dedicate and give oneself to the beloved – 'amour oblatif' – and the desire to possess and subjugate, which he called 'amour captatif'. He considered that those who fell into the second category were especially prone to jealousy. Jealousy is, of course, a universal phenomenon which varies in intensity from the so-called 'normal' to the intensely pathological. This is well attested to in the world's great literature and probably best illustrated in Shakespeare's characterisations of Othello and Leontes; and in more modern works such as those by Tolstoy (see Prins, 1997 for further illustrations).

Protestations of love for, and being loved by, others (who are usually non-attainable individuals) demonstrate these extremes of passion, from the unrequited love of the normal male or female to the pathological protestations and desires of men like Hinckley with his all-consuming passion for Jodie Foster. The boundaries between 'normal' and 'abnormal' are difficult to delineate sharply. Mullen (1991: 593), who has made very significant contributions to the study of pathological love says:

> In our culture jealousy is now regarded not just as problematic or undesirable, but increasingly as unhealthy, as a symptom of immaturity, possessiveness, neurosis and insecurity.

Higgins (1995: 79), a very experienced forensic psychiatrist, also believes that 'the boundary between normal jealousy and morbid jealousy is indistinct':

> Jealousy, or a tendency to be jealous, can be a normal relative transient response in an otherwise well adjusted individual to frank infidelity; a neurotic pre-occupation of a vulnerable and insecure individual; one feature in an individual with a paranoid personality disorder . . . or a frankly delusional idea arising suddenly and unexpectedly either as a single delusional idea or one of a number of related ideas in a typical psychosis.

There is no universal agreement as to aetiology (cause) in cases of 'encapsulated' delusional jealousy. However, a number of explanations have been preferred. For example, the person suffering from the delusion may themselves have behaved promiscuously in the past and have an expectation that the spouse or partner will behave in a similar fashion. Other explanations have embraced the possibility of impotence in the sufferer with consequent projection of a feeling of failure on to the spouse or partner. Freudian and neo-Freudian explanations stress the possibility of repressed homosexuality resulting in fantasies about the male consort of a spouse or partner.

In a recent publication Pines (1998) suggests that 'Although jealousy occurs in different forms and in varying degrees of intensity, it always results from an interaction between a certain predisposition and a particular triggering event'. She considers that predispositions to jealousy vary widely between individuals. For someone with a high predisposition, a triggering event can be as minor as a partner's glance at an attractive stranger passing by. For most people, however, the trigger for intense jealousy is a much more serious event, such as the discovery of an illicit affair. For others, the trigger can be imagined. (As reported by R. Dobson in the *Independent*, 3 September 1998, p. 14; for detailed accounts, see Pines, 1998.)

The irrational nature of the beliefs held by sufferers from this disorder is illustrated in the following three examples:

CASE 1

This is a case described by the nineteenth-century physician Clouston and quoted by Enoch and Trethowan (1979: 47):

> I now have in an asylum two quite rational-looking men, whose chief delusion is that their wives, both women of undoubted character, have been unfaithful to them. Keep them off the subject and they are rational. But on that subject they are utterly delusional and insane.

CASE 2

A more recent case, drawn from the present writer's experience, supports the irrationality of belief so graphically described by Clouston. This concerned a man in his sixties detained in hospital without limit of time (Sections 37/41, Mental Health Act 1983) with a diagnosis of mental illness. He had been charged with the attempted murder of his wife and had a history of infidelity during the marriage. There was a family history of mental illness. The index offence consisted of an attempt to stab his wife to death and a serious assault on his daughter who tried to intervene to protect her. He gave a history of prolonged, but quite unfounded, suspicions of his wife's infidelity. He arranged to have her followed, interrogated her persistently as to her whereabouts (which were always quite innocent) and searched her correspondence and personal belongings for proof of her alleged unfaithfulness. He even inspected her underclothing for signs of seminal staining in order to confirm his delusional beliefs. He also believed that neighbours and others were colluding with his wife to aid her in her unfaithful liaison.

He was regarded as a model patient, well-liked by staff and other residents and, to the unwary and uninformed observer, presented himself as completely rational and reasonable. It was only when asked about his wife that his delusional ideas expressed themselves with terrifying intensity. Although he had been detained in hospital for some years and his delusional ideas were not quite so intrusive as they were on his admission, they were still very easily evoked; the likelihood of his release was remote. His wife had been urged to sever her connections with him entirely and make a new life for herself. However, as is frequently the case, she was reluctant to do so, hoping that her husband's attitude would change.

The wife's attitude is of great importance. This is because in such cases the irrational beliefs held by the sufferer are not easily amenable to treatment; the wife is likely, therefore, to be at considerable risk whenever the offender or offender–patient is released. Some cynical professionals, when asked 'What is the best treatment?', have been known to respond by saying 'Geographical', meaning that the woman would be strongly advised to move home and change her name: it seems that the woman is being doubly victimised. Supervision of these and similar cases requires the utmost vigilance and a capacity to spot subtle changes in both mood and social circumstances. It is well established that many sufferers from delusional jealousy have what the late Dr Murray Cox once described as 'unfinished business' to complete. Even if, sadly, the first victim has died as a result of the delusionally held beliefs, surrogate victims may be found and be similarly at risk. It is important to stress that the management of the delusionally jealous individual has important lessons for the management of other cases where, because of obsessional beliefs, there is an on-going risk of future mayhem.

CASE 3

The third example is an illustration of the manifestation of the disorder in a less severe form. It demonstrates the possibility of improvement through psychotherapeutic intervention and is a personal account, given by Christine Aziz (1987) some years ago, in a national newspaper. Her jealousy, which developed in relation to her partner:

... came unannounced one warm autumn day; a tight pain in the stomach, sweating and nausea. Still cocooned in the intense early days of love, I discovered Simon (her partner) had slept with someone else, and even more hurtful, had denied it. Jealousy had come to stay. The occasional twinge was bearable, but this torment was the surgeon's knife without the anaesthetic. It came unannounced and for hours and evil turned me into a stranger to those who knew and loved me.

In Christine Aziz's case, she was able to realise to some degree that her behaviour was irrational; she was eventually helped through behavioural psychotherapy to deal with it and find some peace of mind.

Erotomania

The notion of pathological (obsessive) possessiveness may assist us in linking pathological jealousy on the one hand, and erotomania on the other. Erotomania (psychose passionelle) is a condition in which the sufferer believes with passionate and irrational conviction that a person, who is usually older and socially quite unattainable (such as an important public figure), is in love with them. The history of the term is well outlined by Enoch and Trethowan (1991) and by Mullen et al. (1993). Concerns about stalking have recently highlighted interest in the condition, notably the harm to victims (Pathe & Mullen, 1997). Taylor et al. (1983) suggest five criteria for making the diagnosis in the female:

1   Presence of the delusion that the woman is loved by a specific man.
2   That the woman has previously had very little contact with this man.
3   That the man is unattainable in some way.
4   That the man nevertheless watches over, protects or follows the woman.
5   That the woman should remain chaste.

Some of these criteria could be applied if the sufferer were male. Taylor and her colleagues found that medication helped their patients to feel more relaxed, but that this did not lead to an early resolution of their amorous beliefs. As with delusional jealousy, the condition is a highly dangerous one, since sufferers may seek to attack those they consider to be rivals for the attentions of those they obsessively love, if they feel the latter has spurned them.

General treatment considerations

Where the conditions described above are the product of some other disturbance (such as organic state, affective disorder, schizophrenic or alcohol related illness) then specific treatments for these conditions may help to alleviate the delusional state. Although Taylor et al. (1983) reported that drugs had some minimal effect, these patients' responses 'to therapeutic approaches were passively co-operative rather than ... [those] ... of active involvement' (see Prins, 1997 for a short account of a variety of treatment methods).

Whatever mode of treatment is adopted, careful questioning of the pathologically jealous individual is essential. Mullen (1996: 240) states:

> The clinician attempting to treat a patient or client in whom jealousy features must keep constantly in mind the possibility of an escalation of conflict producing a resort to violence. Careful and repeated questioning of the jealous individual and their partner is advisable, and, wherever possible, informants outside the relationship should be consulted.

A major concern must be that few treatments seem to offer long-term success. Those that have been reported on are largely based on small sample size, absence of control group and short-term follow-up.

AFFECTIVE DISORDERS AND VIOLENCE

Pale death, the grand physician, cures all pains;
The dead rest well who lived for joys in vain.
John Clare, *Child Harold* 1,215

Affective disorders are characterised by mood changes, in some cases, either abnormally low or abnormally high; these constitute serious depression on the one hand and mania or hypomania on the other. I make no attempt here to indicate some of the other features of these disorders other than as we see them in relation to serious crimes of violence. (See Prins, 1995: 91–4 for a general outline description of signs and symptoms.)

Depression and serious violence

From time to time, one comes across cases in which an individual charged with a serious crime, such as homicide, is found to have been suffering from a major depressive illness at the time of the offence. West (1965: 6), in his classic study of cases of *Murder followed by suicide*, suggested that sufferers from depression of psychotic intensity may:

> become so convinced of the helplessness of their misery that death becomes a happy escape. Sometimes, before committing suicide, they first kill their children and other members of the family . . . Under the delusion of a future without hope and the inevitability of catastrophe overtaking their nearest and dearest as well as themselves, they desire to kill in order to spare their loved ones suffering.

The intensity of such delusional beliefs is also well illustrated by Shipkowensky (1969: 65–6) who stressed that the 'patient feels his personality is without value (delusion of inferiority). His life is without sense, it is only [one of] everlasting suffering; he feels he deserves to be punished for his imaginary crimes.'

CASE 4

AB was a young man in his late twenties. He became so convinced that the world was a terrible place in which to live that he attempted to kill his mother and his sister and so save both of them; he then tried to kill himself. Only swift and fortuitous medical intervention saved all their lives. Following a court appearance for attempted murder, he was made the subject of hospital care; fortunately he responded well to treatment and made an excellent recovery.

Trying to estimate the extent and duration of a severe depressive disorder and its relevance to serious offences such as homicide is very difficult. Gunn et al. (1978: 35) put the problem very clearly:

> It is very difficult to establish *unless several helpful informants are available* whether a depressed murderer is depressed because he has been imprisoned for life, depressed because of the conditions in which he has been imprisoned, depressed by the enormity of his crime, or whether he committed murder because he was depressed in the first place [emphasis added].

This comment by Gunn and his colleagues, about the value of informants, is a very significant one for non-psychiatrically qualified staff; this is because they often have a very important part to play in ensuring that a *comprehensive* social history of the offender/offender–patient is obtained. Often, it is only when this vital information has been gathered that one can see the individual against the background of his or her social milieu, and the strains and stresses within it. Moreover, glimpses of his or her life style against this social background may provide important diagnostic and prognostic clues – a matter of comment in the next two chapters.

There is another potential problem for the psychiatrically unwary. A person who is psychotically depressed may be quite incapable of self-harm or harming others. However, once the worst of the depression begins to lift, they may then have just enough awareness and motivation to put their delusional ideas into effect. The following case, drawn from a non-forensic setting, illustrates this point.

CASE 5

A male patient of 45 had developed all the signs of serious depression over the preceding few months (abnormally high level of anxiety, disturbed sleep pattern, loss of appetite resulting in weight loss and subsequent preoccupation with his bowel function, believing he might have cancer). He took an overdose of sleeping tablets (prescribed by his GP for his insomnia), was admitted to the local hospital and subsequently transferred to a psychiatric unit. Having had some treatment for his depression he felt better; his brother persuaded him to take his discharge (against medical advice). The following evening, he went out alone for a walk, threw himself under a train and was killed.

Finally, Higgins (1990: 348) has another perceptive observation for the unwary:

> Depression may result in serious violence, tension and preoccupation building up over a protracted period and an assault committed in a state of grave psychological turmoil. The act itself might then act as a catharsis, the individual not afterwards appearing depressed nor complaining of depression *and this diagnosis then being missed* [emphasis added].

Manic and hypomanic disorder

> Mad, bad, and dangerous to know
> Lady Caroline Lamb, writing about Byron

The cardinal features of mania (or, most frequently, hypomania) are the very opposite of those seen in depressive disorder. Activities are speeded up, the sufferer becomes overexcited, demonstrates a euphoric mood, has grandiose but wholly unrealistic plans for their future, becomes irritable and disinhibited, does not eat or sleep because they are too 'busy' to do so, and will brook no interference from others in their activities. It is this latter attribute that makes them potentially highly dangerous.

CASE 6

A young woman became increasingly convinced that members of the Cabinet were her close friends and would assist her in her grandiose schemes for the development of a quite unrealistic business enterprise. When her calls to Downing Street were not reciprocated, she became increasingly angry and threatened those she saw as obstructing her, with physical violence. She was quite without insight, did not believe that she might be ill, and because of her threats to others she was compulsorily hospitalised. Following treatment by medication her mood became slightly less high, though she remained very irritable, somewhat disinhibited, and showed little insight. It was envisaged that she would need to remain in hospital for some time until her mood stabilised and her preoccupations diminished.

The characteristics of this type of patient or offender–patient are worth re-emphasising since such persons justify the 'illness' label very clearly. They consider themselves to be omnipotent and become convinced that their wildest ideas are, in fact, entirely practical. Because there is no impairment of memory, they are capable of giving persuasive rational-ised arguments and explanations to support their actions. It is very important to stress that such persons are very difficult to treat without compulsion since they resist the idea that anything is wrong with them. However, though lacking insight, they can appear deceptively lucid and rational; it is this that makes their behaviour a very real risk to others. As already noted, they can be not only hostile, but also physically aggressive to those they think are obstructing them in their plans and activities. Persons in full-flight hypomania can be some of the most potentially dangerous people suffering from a definable mental illness.

SEVERE PERSONALITY DISORDER AND VIOLENCE

> A devil, a born devil, on whose nature
> Nurture can never stick; on whom my pains
> Humanely taken, all, all lost, quite lost.
> *The Tempest*, IV, i

The severely personality disordered (psychopathic) illustrate very clearly some of the problems already referred to in defining mental disorders. Because there is often dispute as to whether such persons are suffering from a mental disorder at all within the meaning of the 1983 Mental Health Act, or whether they are treatable or not, there is good reason for using the term 'mental disturbance' to describe the condition from which they suffer or, more likely, make others suffer.

As I write this chapter, the deliberations of a joint Home Office and Department of Health working group on the future management of severely personality disordered individuals (psychopathically disordered) are awaited. An additional report of the inquiry into the Personality Disorder Unit at Ashworth (Special) Hospital has also reported (Fallon et al., 1999). The inquiry team has proffered opinions as to the most effective systems of disposal and management. I have been struck by the very real and anxious concerns expressed by those in the front line concerning the clients 'nobody wants to know'. 'Nobody' in this context usually means a perceived reluctance on the part of the psychiatric services to deal with such people. Resource constraints have led most general psychiatrists to become much more circumspect, nay reluctant, to offer treatment for a group of people they regard as untreatable. However, there have been some notable exceptions, particularly amongst forensic psychiatrists (see, for example, Bailey & MacCulloch, 1992). In the penal sphere, there has been a compounding adverse influence, largely generated by the 'nothing works' policies of the early 1970s. This penal nihilism has found support in certain 'exclusionist' political views and, from the management aspect, by prison overcrowding. Thus, the two services that might have provided management and support for this admittedly very difficult group of people, have been reluctant to do so.

I now deal with the following matters: (1) brief historical context; (2) aetiological considerations; and (3) some aspects of management in the light of current knowledge.

Historical context

Most readers will be familiar with the history of the development of the condition we know today as psychopathic disorder. (For detailed accounts see Dolan & Coid, 1993; Berrios in Tyrer & Stein, 1992; and Prins, 1995, Chapter 5.) The French psychiatrist Pinel (1806) is usually given the credit for the first description of the characteristics we currently regard as psychopathic. However, analysis of Pinel's work would suggest that he probably included a number of cases we would not regard today as falling within the modern classification. In the 1830s, the English psychiatrist and anthropologist Prichard (1835: 135) formulated the well-known concept of 'moral insanity' which he described as follows:

> A madness, consisting of a morbid perversion of the natural feelings, affections, inclinations, temper, habits, moral dispositions and natural impulses, without any remarkable disorder or defect of the intellect or knowing or reasoning faculties, and particularly without any insane illusion or hallucination.

It is important to place Prichard's often quoted remarks in context. To Prichard, the term 'moral' meant emotional and psychological and was not intended to denote the opposite of immoral. In the 1880s the concept of constitutional psychopathy became popular, being much in line with current thinking about the interest in hereditary factors in the aetiology of criminality. The beginning of the twentieth century saw the introduction of the terms 'moral defective' and 'moral imbecile', both finding expression in the Mental Deficiency Act 1913. In the 1930s, interest developed in neurological factors and the relevance of illnesses such as encephalitis, epilepsy and chorea to psychopathic behaviour. Subsequently, psychoanalytic explanations of the disorder became popular; these were followed by a reawakening of interest in more socially generated explanations – as evidenced in the USA, with that country's use of the term 'sociopath'. The term 'psychopathic disorder' found its way into England and Wales legislation in the Mental Health Act of 1959, where it was defined in Section 4(4) as:

> A persistent disorder or disability of mind (whether or not including subnormality of intelligence) which results in abnormally aggressive or seriously irresponsible conduct on the part of the patient concerned *and requires or is susceptible to treatment* [emphasis added].

The development of a more circumspect view of treatability referred to above found expression in the revised definition of psychopathic disorder in the 1983 Mental Health Act (Section 1 (2)) as follows:

> A persistent disorder or disability of mind (whether or not including significant impairment of intelligence) which results in abnormally aggressive or seriously irresponsible conduct on the part of the person concerned.

The question of treatability does not appear in the new definition, but finds expression in Section 37(2)(i) as follows: '. . . and in the case of psychopathic disorder . . . that such treatment is likely to *alleviate or prevent a deterioration of his condition*' [emphasis added].

The usefulness of the term 'psychopathic' was considered by the Committee on Mentally Disordered Offenders (Butler Committee) in their report (HO and DHSS, 1975), and in more recent years the nature and management of the disorder was re-considered by a Department of Health and Home Office Working Group chaired by Dr John Reed. (DOH & HO, 1994). Its list of 28 recommendations includes a plea for more and better quality research, the introduction of a 'hybrid order' referred to in Chapter 2, and the replacement of the term 'psychopathic' in the 1983 Act. It would be replaced by 'personality disorder' which would not be further defined. The Working Group also considered that a wide range of options should continue to be made available for those judged to be severely personality disordered (psychopathic). It is worth noting at this point, that the term 'psychopathic disorder' is not to be found in either the Northern Ireland or the Scottish mental health legislation. They seem to manage satisfactorily without it. Perhaps England and Wales should explore their experience more closely.

In summary, it is possible to trace three important themes in the development of the concept: *first*, as Coid (1993) suggests, the notion of an abnormal personality as defined by social maladjustment, originating in France and further developed powerfully in the UK, leading to the current legal definition of psychopathic disorder (see above); *second*, a concept also originating in France, which was influenced by the notion of mental degeneracy; persons so afflicted were considered to have fragile personalities; and *third*, the German notion of defining abnormal (psychopathic) personality types. In brief, over the years approaches to the personality disordered (including psychopathic disorder at the far end of the spectrum) have been characterised by: the *traditional psychiatric*; *the postulation of some basic psychological deficiency*; the *social deviance or social competence model*; and, in more recent years, *neuro-psychophysiological approaches*. From a *clinical*, as distinct from a *legal* point of view, the term 'psychopathic disorder' does not find much favour. Neither of the two major classificatory psychiatric texts (the APA's *DSM – IV* and WHO's *ICD – 10*) uses the term. The former uses the term Anti-Social Personality Disorder and the latter Dissocial Personality Disorder. It is very important for academics and practitioners to appreciate that whatever form they use, it is likely to be influenced by prevailing notions of morality and responsibility (Treves-Brown: 1977).

From the practitioner's point of view, Coid (1989: 750) states that although 'there is still little agreement on the nature of the conditions encompassed by the term . . . it is a concept that remains at the core of clinical practice in forensic psychiatry'. Over the years, contributions to the debate about the disorder have come from within and without the profession of psychiatry; few disciplines have been held to lack relevance to such discussion. Acute observations have come from social scientists and lawyers. Many criminal justice and mental health professionals must have felt beleaguered by those who have suggested that the disorder they were trying to treat was in fact a 'non-condition' in the medical sense. Many years ago, Baroness Wootton pointed out the dangers of the circular arguments that bedevil our understanding of the condition; specifying 'the circular process by which mental abnormality is inferred from anti-social behaviour while anti-social behaviour is explained by mental abnormality' (Wootton, 1959: 250). Despite continuing concerns about the viability of the concept, penal and mental health professionals are asked to assess, and sometimes to try to manage, such people. Tyrer (1989: 240) has suggested rather wittily that 'the diagnosis of personality disorder is similar to an income tax form; it is unpleasant and unwanted, but cannot be avoided in psychiatric practice'. Rather more positively, Gunn (1992: 202) suggests that 'clusters of personality problems that amount to clinical syndromes should be treated as such and not discriminated against'. Others have condemned the concept as currently framed, suggesting that it is no less than a moral judgement pretending to be a diagnosis (see, for example, Lewis, 1974; Blackburn, 1993; Lewis & Appleby, 1988; and Cavadino, 1998).

Aetiology

The search for causes has as long a history as the concept itself. These have included genetic and hereditary predisposition, cortical disturbance and immaturity and close familial and environmental influences. Dolan and Coid (1993) stressed the need for continuing research into environmental *and* constitutional aspects. Coid (1993: 156) advocates caution in espousing the notion of psychopathic disorder as a single entity:

> The sheer complexity and range of psychopathology in psychopathic disorder has previously led to the suggestion that these individuals could be considered to suffer from a series of conditions that would

best be subsumed under a broad generic term 'psychopathic disorders' rather than a single entity . . . This would have two immediate advantages. Firstly, it demarcates a poorly defined area that requires further empirical research and where future developments are unlikely to come from a purely trait-based concept of the relevant psychopathology. Secondly, it aligns these syndromes to the legal concept of 'psychopathic disorder' within the MHA 1983.

This latter observation seems important in relation to current controversies over the treatability of detained patients alleged to be suffering from psychopathic disorder. As I write, a detained offender–patient has won the right (on appeal to the High Court) to a fresh Mental Health Review Tribunal on the grounds that he is untreatable. It is alleged that an earlier Tribunal hearing gave inadequate reasons for their decision to continue his detention (*Independent*, 16 September 1998, p. 4).

Interest has revived recently concerning possible organic causes for the condition, including both major and minor cerebral insults in infancy and in the consequences of obstetric complications. However, this is not to deny the powerful influence of the environment. It may well be, as with disorders such as the schizophrenias, that it is the interplay of social forces and pressures acting on an already vulnerable personality (for whatever reason) that may tend to produce the condition. The highly complicated and sophisticated neuro–physio–chemical research undertaken in recent years fosters speculation that *some* of the answers to the problems of aetiology may eventually be found in the area of brain biochemistry. Certainly, one cannot ignore the evidence, admittedly laboratory-based, of such factors as low anxiety thresholds, cortical immaturity, frontal lobe damage and, perhaps most relevant of all, the *true* (as distinct from the wrongly labelled) psychopath's need for excitement – the achievement of a 'high'. (For a useful summary of recent research see Skett & Stepney, 1995.) This is described very graphically in Wambaugh's book about Colin Pitchfork (Wambaugh, 1989). Pitchfork was convicted of the rape and murder of two teenage girls in Leicestershire during the period 1983–86. In interviews with the police, it is alleged he stated that he obtained a 'high' from the knowledge that his victims or likely victims were virginal. He also described an additional aspect of his excitement, namely obtaining sex outside marriage. As with others assessed as psychopathic, he also demonstrated a great degree of charm; for example, he was able to get his wife to forgive him for a number of instances of admitted unfaithfulness.

Some key characteristics

Some aspects of these have already been alluded to. I now make further brief comment. Sir Martin Roth, the doyen of British psychiatry, has stated what he regards as some of the key features of those demonstrating psychopathic disorder. He suggests these are egotism, immaturity in various manifestations, aggressiveness, low frustration tolerance, and the inability to learn from experience so that social demands and expectations are never met (Roth, 1990). This brief list encapsulates many of the more detailed characteristics suggested by Cleckley in the various editions of his seminal work *The mask of sanity* (Cleckley, 1976; see also Hare, 1993). To these items one should add the following three elements: *first*, the *curious super-ego lacunae*, rather than the total lack of conscience suggested by some workers; *second*, the greater than usual need for excitement and arousal already referred to; *third*, a capacity to create chaos among family, friends, and those involved in trying to manage or contain them. I would suggest that this last characteristic is one of the most accurate indicators of the *true*, as distinct from the pejoratively labelled, psychopath. Maybe it is this element of the chaotic that carries with it the impression of quite remorseless behaviour that is coupled with gratuitousness and complete lack of justification. Johns and Quay (1962) graphically stated the lack of true feeling content over thirty years ago in their perceptive comment that psychopaths 'know the words but not the music'. Rieber and Green (quoted by Vetter in Egger, 1990) suggest four salient characteristics: thrill-seeking, pathological glibness, anti-social pursuit of power, and absence of guilt (Vetter in Egger, 1990: 81). They give great prominence, as I do, to the phenomenon of thrill-seeking. Rieber and Green 'describe the psychopath as performing a Mephisto Waltz on the tightrope of danger' (quoted by Vetter in Egger 1990: 82). It is as though this is necessary to fill the emotional void so often encountered in the psychopathic. This internal emptiness has also been stressed by Whiteley (1994: 16), who quotes a former patient writing to him from prison:

> I thought everything I said, did and thought was not real, that I was not real, almost as though I did not exist, so I could never affect anyone because I was not real, no-one could possibly take me seriously because I was not real.

Does the concept assist in management?

Describing and trying to delineate a disorder, has the advantage of hopefully setting some boundaries to it and helping to create typologies that may assist in management, even if the latter is difficult and may frequently result in failure. I believe there *is* value in the concept, provided we are not too all-inclusive in its use, and misuse it as an escape from working with such people. Maier (1990: 766) puts the problem very neatly, when, describing the reluctance of – in this instance – psychiatrists to deal with psychopathically disordered individuals, he says:

> Could it be after all these Freudian years, that psychiatrists have denied the hatred they feel for psychopaths and criminals, and thus have been unable to treat psychopaths adequately because their conceptual basis for treatment has been distorted by unconscious, denied feelings from the start?

This implied need for self-inspection was also outlined in an earlier contribution by another psychiatrist, Treves-Brown (1977: 62) who wrote:

> As long as a doctor believes that the psychopaths are mostly 'bad', his successful treatment rate will be dismal. Since it takes two to form a relationship, an outside observer could be forgiven for suspecting that a doctor who describes a patient as unable to form a relationship is simply justifying his own hostility to this patient.

Although these statements are by psychiatrists, the lessons can be applied to other professionals who may have to deal with those adjudged to be exhibiting psychopathic disorder in some form or another, and whose behaviour so often places others at so much risk.

Some empirical evidence

A few years ago, some colleagues and I sought the opinions of three groups of professionals (psychiatrists, psychologists, and probation officers) on two topics. *First*: was the concept of psychopathic disorder useful? *Second*: did they think psychopathic disorder was a treatable condition? Space does not permit a detailed presentation of our methodology and findings; these have been described fully elsewhere (see Tennent et al., 1990; 1993). Despite a somewhat limited response rate to our questionnaires, we found our respondents considered that the concept of psychopathic disorder was a useful one. We also found that *psychiatrists'* opinions about psychopathic disorder have remained very constant. As to *treatability*, we again had to form our judgements on a limited response rate. However, our modest findings suggested that although few clear-cut views emerged as to the *best* treatment modalities, there were clearer indications as to those felt to be unhelpful. It would seem that there were *higher* expectations of treatment efficacy with symptoms such as 'chronically antisocial', 'abnormally aggressive', and 'lacking control over impulses' and much *lower* expectations for symptoms such as 'inability to experience guilt', 'lack of remorse or shame' and 'pathological egocentricity'.

Support for our findings can be found in a later and more extensive survey of all forensic psychiatrists working in Regional Secure Units, Special Hospitals and other forensic settings in England, Scotland and Wales. Cope (1993) achieved a response rate of 91 per cent. The majority of the psychiatrists responding to her questionnaire were in favour of offering treatment to psychopaths; only about 10 per cent believed that psychopaths were untreatable. There was considerable support for setting up specialised units for treating psychopathically disordered patients, especially in prisons and special hospitals. Some support for the foregoing may be found in recent work reported from Canada. In a review of a number of studies, Hare et al. (1993:175–6) conclude that:

> [These] . . . studies provide considerable support for the validity of the psychopathic construct, its strong association with crime and violence and consequently, its importance to the criminal justice and correctional systems.

Management issues

Management should be viewed against the contextual background already outlined and the need to keep our prejudices in check – for these clients/offenders/patients are truly the 'degenerate, not nice, unrewarding' offenders described so graphically by the late Dr Peter Scott (1975: 8). Earlier, Scott (1960: 1645) also pointed out that 'some workers intuitively obtain good results with certain psychopaths' and he went on to say that 'it should be possible to find out how they do it'. This statement has been echoed more recently in a contribution on psychotherapy for personality disorder by Higgitt and Fonagy. (1993: 253), who state that 'Therapist commitment and enthusiasm appears to be of special significance and subjective aspects of patient–therapist 'fit' (complementarity) may be particularly important for this group of patients' (see also Tyrer, 1998). Three aspects of these matters are now considered.

First   Those psychopathically disordered individuals whose behaviour is marked by serious episodes of aggression and violence should be carefully assessed and monitored for possible organic causes of their behaviour (see Miller, 1999). This is especially important if their persistent violence seems to be unprovoked or minimally provoked by others and associated with the ingestion of even small amounts of alcohol and/or other drugs. It may be that they can be helped by *carefully monitored and controlled* amounts of medication. Stein (1993) has written an excellent detailed review of the extent and limitations of drug treatments in the management of personality disorders. I am not advocating medicating people without the most scrupulous care and attention, for I know of too many situations where medication may have been used unwisely to suggest anything to the contrary.

Second   There appears to be some evidence to suggest that even some apparently intractable cases can be helped to behave more appropriately over time. It may be in these cases (and particularly in those that also show some history of aggressive outbursts) that their impulsivity tends to diminish with advancing years. Intensive psycho-analytic therapy does not seem to be particularly successful in such cases. Calm confrontation over prolonged periods of their adverse behaviour (as it affects themselves and others) may help to bring about change. Some workers advocate that this is best carried out in peer-group situations, but benefit can also accrue from one-to-one encounters. Whether this work is carried out on a group or individual basis, it is *essential* for workers not to feel *personally* affronted at being misled, lied to, evaded or made to feel helpless in the face of the chaos I referred to earlier. It is a question of possessing *extreme patience* in dealing with such people. The late George Lyward, who was a gifted worker with severely maladjusted youths (some of whom were possibly psychopaths in embryo) once made the telling remark that 'patience is love that can wait'. It is this capacity to tolerate fear, hate, hostility, manipulation and 'splitting' that is often so vital for any degree of progress, however small. Fifty years ago Winnicott had some wise words in this context. Writing of the problems involved in dealing with 'hard to like' patients he said:

> However much he loves his patients he cannot avoid hating them and fearing them and the better he knows this the less will hate and fear be the motives determining what he does for his patients.
>
> (Winnicott, 1949: 71)

Third   when one examines the varieties of approaches that have been tried with psychopathically disordered individuals, it has always seemed to me that there are three key words that come to mind in trying to deal with them. These are *consistence, persistence* and *insistence*. Perhaps it is also wise to remember the words of the writer Zamyatin in his novel *We* (1920), 'Man is like a novel; one doesn't know until the very last page how the thing will end.'

It will be necessary to retain the *concept* of psychopathic disorder (or whatever *title* it may come to be replaced by), provided we accept and adopt the caveats I have outlined. In addition, we shall move towards a better understanding and management of this most difficult group of people only if we endeavour to rid ourselves of our preconceptions and prejudices and adopt a professional stance. This will not be easy because 'it is in this area of affective, subjective, empathic understanding that . . . suspicions and fears arise' (Cordess, 1993: 424). However, if we succeed, we may eventually improve our skills in managing one of the most enigmatic and problematic groups of people known to the criminal justice, penal and mental health care services.

CONCLUDING COMMENTS

Despite advances in research methods the connections between various forms of mental disturbance and serious violence are by no means clear cut. However, there *is* reasonable evidence to demonstrate that certain forms of serious mental disturbance (such as the functional psychoses, certain allied conditions and personality disorder (psychopathy)) *do* have a raised relationship. Reed (1995: 6) makes four observations about these links. I have paraphrased these as they seem to sum up the position very succinctly (see also Howlett, 1998: 90–6):

1   Most mentally ill people and the learning disabled do not present an increased risk of violence to others.[5]
2   The best predictors of future offending behaviour for the mentally disordered are similar to those found in non-mentally disordered populations: prior offence records, history of family criminality and poor parenting experiences.
3   People with functional psychosis present an increased risk of harm to others when they have active symptoms; the more so if they are also substance abusers.
4   By definition, people designated as showing severe personality disorder (psychopathy) present an increased risk to others.[6]

Of cardinal significance is the fact that social and environmental factors will influence both onset and course of severe mental disturbances. Mental health and criminal justice professionals need to be highly aware of this. In a number of cases, trigger factors, and environmental hazards have not been recognised and dealt with as effectively as they might have been. For this reason inquiries into such situations form the basis of the next chapter.

Combining an actuarial and clinical perspective, Bowden (1996: 24), states:

> A narrative explanation will tell us that in certain necessary conditions (e.g. certain types of delusions and affective states) violence *can* happen; it would not tell us that it is inevitable (in which case the behaviour would not be unexpected). Repetitiveness can lead from possibility to probability explanation, but it is the introspectibles (meanings and reasons) which help us to see why some actions are highly probable.

Some aspects of these meanings and reasons are explored in the final chapter of this book.

Hiday (1997) provides an extensive algorithmic view of the topic. She stresses that although sophisticated and methodologically sound studies have found an association between severe mental illnesses and violence, this association has been presented by responsible researchers in qualified terms in three ways: (a) the association is a modest one; (b) 'the mentally ill account for only a very small proportion of the total violence in society'; and (c) only those with major mental illness and active psychotic symptoms demonstrate higher rates of violence. She also makes the very important point that 'the paths between mental illness and violence are mainly indirect and contingent' and that the links are complex and multiple (p. 410).[7]

Bearing in mind some of the concerns expressed in Chapter 1 about the influence of the media and 'moral panics' it seems important to place the relationship between serious mental disorder (notably schizophrenia) and violence into perspective. Dyer (1998: 74) concludes that: '95 per cent of homicides are committed by people without schizophrenia . . . one would therefore expect about 35 homicides in England and Wales annually to be committed by people with schizophrenia and in Scotland three to four per year.' These small numbers should also be set against the figures for the total number of persons indicted for homicide in England and Wales between 1990 and 1995 (see Table 3.3).

Table 3.3 Number of persons indicted for homicide[a] (England and Wales)
1990–95

1990	623
1991	703
1992	699
1993	674
1994	623
1995	399[b]

Source: Home Office (1996: 83).

Notes
a Figures include convictions for murder, manslaughter and infanticide.
b The figure for 1995 is incomplete; final numbers were not available at the time of compilation.

Gunn (1996: 117) adds a broader cautionary note. He suggests that we can expect about fifty people per year to be killed by those suffering from psychosis:

> Thus, throughout the world many hundreds of people are killed by psychotic patients each year. In other words, the age-old fear that patients who have gone mad might turn violent is probably based upon an understanding of the potential horror of psychosis. The important thing is to keep this in perspective. Saying that 11 per cent of men charged with homicide suffer from schizophrenia is a very long way from saying that a high proportion of patients with schizophrenia commit violence.

NOTES

1 For a comprehensive and varied discussion of aspects of the relationship between mental disturbance generally and serious mental disturbance in particular and violence, see the collection of papers edited by Peay (1998), notably Parts I and V.
2 The full definitions are as follows in Section 1(2) of the Act:

> 'Mental Disorder' means mental illness, arrested or incomplete development of mind, psychopathic disorder and any other disorder or disability of mind and 'mentally disordered' shall be construed accordingly;

> 'Mental Impairment' means a state of arrested or incomplete development of mind (not amounting to severe mental impairment) which

includes significant impairment of intelligence and social functioning and is associated with *abnormally aggressive or seriously irresponsible conduct* on the part of the person concerned and 'mentally impaired' shall be construed accordingly [emphasis added];

'Psychopathic Disorder' means persistent disorder or disability of mind (whether or not including significant impairment of intelligence) which results in abnormally aggressive or seriously irresponsible conduct on the part of the person concerned.

3 It should be noted that the Mental Health Act expressly excludes the compulsory detention of persons as mentally disordered 'by reason only of promiscuity or other immoral conduct, sexual deviancy or dependence on alcohol or drugs' (Section 1(3)).

4 It is important to note that by no means all special hospital patients are *offender*–patients. About one third are detained because their behaviour has been too dangerous and disruptive to be coped with in ordinary psychiatric hospitals or units.

5 Most mentally ill people present a greater risk *to themselves* by acts of self-harm. For a recent review of the relationship between violent *offending* and psychiatric disorder, see Mitchell (1999).

6 It is relevant here to stress the importance of co-morbidity. For example, a person demonstrating psychopathic disorder can develop a psychotic illness such as depression.

7 Readers wishing to explore aspects of management further should consult Peay (1998, Part V); Widiger and Trull (1994); and Prins (1993).

REFERENCES

American Psychiatric Association. (1994). *Diagnostic and statistical manual of mental disorders* (4th ed.). Washington, DC: Author (APA).

Aziz, C. (1987, 10 November). Prey to the green-eyed monster. *Independent*, p. 15.

Bailey, J. & McCulloch, M. (1992). Patterns of convictions in patients discharged directly into the community from a Special Hospital. *Journal of Forensic Psychiatry*, *3*, 445–61.

Banay, R.S. (1942). Alcoholism and crime. *Quarterly Journal of Studies in Alcohol*, *2*, 686–716.

Banks, C. (1964). *Studies in psychology*. London: University of London Press.

Belfrage, H. (1998). A ten-year follow-up of criminality in Stockholm mental patients: New evidence for a relation between mental disorder and crime. *British Journal of Criminology*, *38*, 145–55.

Berrios, G. (1993). Personality disorders: A conceptual history. In P. Tyrer & G. Stein (eds), *Personality disorder reviewed*. London: Gaskell.

Birmingham, L., Mason, D., & Grubin, D. (1996). Prevalence of mental disorder in remand prisoners: Consecutive case study. *British Medical Journal, 313*, 1521–4.

Birmingham, L., Mason, D., & Grubin, D. (1998). A follow-up study of mentally disordered men remanded to prison. *Criminal Behaviour and Mental Health, 8*, 202–13.

Blackburn, R. (1993). *The psychology of criminal conduct: Theory, research and practice.* Chichester: Wiley.

Bland, R.C., Newman, S.C., Thompson, A.H., & Dyck, R.J. (1998). Psychiatric disorders in the population and in prisons. *International Journal of Law and Psychiatry, 21*, 273–9.

Bluglass, R.S. (1966). *A psychiatric study of Scottish prisoners.* Unpublished MD thesis, University of Aberdeen.

Bowden, P. (1996). Violence and mental disorder. In N. Walker, (ed.), *Dangerous people.* London: Blackstone Press.

Brooke, D., Taylor, C., Gunn, J., & Maden, A. (1996). Point prevalence study of mental disorder in unconvicted male prisoners in England and Wales. *British Medical Journal, 313*, 1524–7.

Bromberg, L.W., & Thompson, C.B. (1937). The relation of psychosis, mental defect and personality type to crime. *Journal of Criminal Law and Criminology, 28*, 70–89.

Cavadino, M. (1998). Death to the psychopath. *Journal of Forensic Psychiatry, 9*, 5–8.

Cleckley, H. (1976). *The mask of sanity* (5th ed.). St. Louis: C.V. Mosby.

Coid, J.W. (1989). Personality disorders. *Current opinion in psychiatry, 2*, 750–6.

Coid, J. (1993). Current concepts and classifications of psychopathic disorder. In P. Tyrer & G. Stein (eds), *Personality disorder reviewed.* London: Gaskell Books.

Cope, R. (1993). A survey of forensic psychiatrists' views on psychopathic disorder. *Journal of Forensic Psychiatry, 4*, 214–35.

Cordess, C. (1993). Understanding, exoneration and condemnation. *Journal of Forensic Psychiatry, 4*, 423–6.

Cramer, M.J., & Blacker, E.J. (1963). 'Early' and 'Late' problem drinkers among female prisoners. *Journal of Health and Human Behaviour, 4*, 282–90.

Day, K. (1993). Crime and mental retardation: A review. In K. Howells & C.R. Hollin (eds), *Clinical approaches to the mentally disordered offender,* Chichester: Wiley.

Day, K. (1997). Sex offenders with learning disabilities. In S.G. Read (ed.), *Psychiatry and learning disability.* London: Saunders.

Department of Health & Home Office (1994). *Report of the working group on psychopathic disorder* (Chairman, Dr John Reed, CB). London: Author.

Dolan, B., & Coid, J. (1993). *Psychopathic and anti-social personality disorders.* London: Gaskell Books.

Dyer, J.A.T. (1998). Treatment in the community in the absence of consent. *Psychiatric Bulletin, 22*, 74–6.

Enoch, M., & Trethowan, W. (1979). *Uncommon psychiatric syndromes* (2nd ed.). Bristol: John Wright.

Enoch, M., & Trethowan, W. (1991). *Uncommon psychiatric syndromes* (3rd ed.). London: Butterworth-Heinemann.

Fallon, P., QC, Bluglass, R., Edwards, B., & Daniels, G. (1999). *Report of the committee of inquiry into the personality disorder unit, Ashworth Special Hospital*. Cmnd 4194(1) and (2). Plus executive summary. London: Stationery Office.

Faulk, M. (1976). A psychiatric study of men serving sentences in Winchester prison. *Medicine, Science and the Law, 16*, 244–51.

Freeman, H. (1991). The human brain and political behaviour. *British Journal of Psychiatry, 159*, 19–32.

Gibbens, T.C.N., & Silverman, M. (1970). Alcoholism among prisoners. *Pscyhological Medicine, 1*, 73–8.

Gillies, H. (1965). Murder in the west of Scotland. *British Journal of Psychiatry, 111*, 1087–94.

Glueck, B. (1918). A study of 608 admissions to Sing Sing prison. *Mental Hygiene, 2*, 85–151.

Gunn, J. (1973). *A psychiatric study of offenders in the south-east region of England*. Unpublished manuscript.

Gunn, J. (1977). Criminal behaviour and mental disorders. *British Journal of Psychiatry, 130*, 317–29.

Gunn, J. (1992). Personality disorders and forensic psychiatry. *Criminal Behaviour and Mental Health, 2*, 202–11.

Gunn, J. (1996). The management and discharge of violent patients. In N. Walker (ed.), *Dangerous people*. London: Blackstone Press.

Gunn, J., Robertson, G., Dell, S., & Way C. (1978). *Psychiatric aspects of imprisonment*. London: Academic Press.

Gunn, J., Maden, A., & Swinton, M. (1991a). Treatment needs of prisoners with psychiatric disorders. *British Medical Journal, 303*, 338–41.

Gunn, J., Maden, A., & Swinton, M. (1991b). *Mentally disordered prisoners*. London: Home Office.

Guze, S.B. (1976). *Criminality and psychiatric disorders*. Oxford: Oxford University Press.

Hare, R.D. (1993). *Without conscience: The disturbing world of the psychopath among us*. London: Pocket Books.

Hare, R.D., Strachan, C.E., & Forth, A.E. (1993). Psychopathy and crime: A review. In K. Howells & C.R. Hollin (eds), *Clinical approaches to the mentally disordered offender*. Chichester: Wiley.

Hiday, V.A. (1997). Understanding the connection between mental illness and violence. *International Journal of Law and Psychiatry, 20*, 399–417.

Higgins, J. (1990). Affective disorders. In R. Bluglass & P. Bowden (eds), *Principles and practice of forensic psychiatry*. London: Churchill Livingstone.

Higgins, J. (1995). Crime and mental disorder II: Forensic aspects of psychiatric disorder. In D. Chiswick & R. Cope (eds), *Seminars in practical forensic psychiatry*. London: Gaskell Books.

Higgitt, A. and Fonagy, P. (1993). Psychotherapy in borderline and narcissistic personality disorders. In P. Tyrer & G. Stein (eds), *Personality disorder reviewed*. London: Gaskell Books.

Hodgins, S. (1992). Mental disorder, intellectual deficiency and crime. *Archives of General Psychiatry, 49*, 476–83.

Hodgins, S. (1995). Major mental disorder and criminality. *Psychology, Crime and Law, 2*, 5–17.

Home Office, & Department of Health and Social Security. (1975). *Report of the committee on mentally abnormal offenders* (Chairman, Lord Butler of Saffron Walden, Cmnd 6244). London: HMSO.

Home Office, & Department of Health. (1991). *Review of health and social services for mentally disordered offenders and others requiring similar services: steering committee* (Chairman, Dr John Reed, CB), *Reports of the service advisory groups with glossary*. London: Author.

Home Office. (1996). *Criminal statistics for England and Wales* (Cmnd 3421). London: HMSO.

Howlett, M. (1998). *Medication, non-compliance and mentally disordered offenders*. London: Zito Trust.

Humphreys, M., Johnstone, E., & McMillan, F. (1994). Offending among first episode schizophrenics. *Journal of Forensic Psychiatry, 5*, 51–61.

Johns, J.H., & Quay, H.C. (1962). The effect of social reward and verbal conditioning in psychopathic and neurotic military offenders. *Journal of Consulting Psychology, 26*, 217–20.

Lagache, D. (1947). *La jalousie amoureuse*. Paris: Presses Universitaires de France.

Lewis, Sir A. (1974). Psychopathic personality: A most elusive category. *Psychological Medicine, 4*, 133–44.

Lewis, G., & Appleby, L. (1988). Personality disorders: The patients psychiatrists dislike. *British Journal of Psychiatry, 153*, 44–9.

Lindquist, P., & Allebeck, P. (1990). Schizophrenia and crime: A longitudinal follow-up of 644 schizophrenics in Stockholm. *British Journal of Psychiatry, 157*, 345–50.

Link, B.J., Andrews, H., & Cullen, F.T. (1992). The violent and illegal behaviour of mental patients reconsidered. *American Sociological Review, 57*, 275–92.

Link, B.J., & Steuve, A. (1994). Psychotic symptoms and violent/illegal behaviour of mental patients compared to community controls. In J. Monahan & H.J. Steadman (eds), *Violence and mental disorder: Developments in risk assessment*. Chicago and London: University of Chicago Press.

Maier, G.J. (1990). Psychopathic disorders: Beyond countertransference. *Current Opinion in Psychiatry, 3*, 766–9.

Marshall, J. (1998). Dual diagnosis: Co-morbidity of severe mental illness and substance misuse. *Journal of Forensic Psychiatry*, *9*, 9–15.

Maule, H.G., & Cooper, J. (1996). Alcoholism and crime: A study of drinking habits of 50 discharged prisoners. *British Journal of Addiction*, *61*, 201–12.

McNeil, D.E., Binder, R., & Greenfield, T. (1988). Predictions of violence in civilly committed acute psychiatric patients. *American Journal of Psychiatry*, *145*, 965–70.

Miller, E. (1999). Head injury and offending. *Journal of Forensic Psychiatry*, *10*, 157–66.

Mitchell, E.W. (1999). Does psychiatric disorder affect the likelihood of violent offending? A critique of the major findings. *Medicine, Science and the Law*, *39*, 23–30.

Modestin, J., & Ammann, R. (1995). Mental disorders and criminal behaviour. *British Journal of Psychiatry*, *166*, 667–75.

Monahan, J. (1992). Mental disorder and violent behaviour: Perceptions and evidence. *American Psychologist*, *74*, 511–21.

Mullen, P. (1981). Jealousy: The pathology of passion. *British Journal of Psychiatry*, *158*, 593–601.

Mullen, P. (1996). Jealousy and the emergence of violent and intimidatory behaviours. *Criminal Behaviour and Mental Health*, *6*, 194–205.

Mullen, P., Taylor, P.J., & Wesseley, S. (1993). Psychosis, violence and crime. In J. Gunn and P.J. Taylor (eds), *Forensic psychiatry: Clinical, legal and ethical issues*, London: Butterworth-Heinemann.

Mullen, P., & Pathe, M. (1994). Stalking and the pathologies of love. *Australian and New Zealand Journal of Psychiatry*, *28*, 469–77.

National Association for the Care and Resettlement of Offenders. (1993). *Community care and mentally disordered offenders* (Policy Paper No. 1, Mental Health Advisory Committee: Chairman, H. Prins). London: Author (NACRO).

Oltman, J.E., & Friedman, S. (1941). A psychiatric study of one hundred criminals. *Journal of Nervous and Mental Diseases*, *93*, 16–41.

Pathe, M., & Mullen, P. (1997). The impact of stalkers on their victims. *British Journal of Psychiatry*, *170*, 12–17.

Peay, J. (ed.). (1998). *Criminal justice and the mentally disordered*. Dartmouth: Ashgate Press.

Pinel, P.H. (1806). *A treatise on insanity*. New York: Hafner.

Pines, A.M. (1998). *Romantic jealousy: Causes, symptoms and cures*. London: Routledge.

Prichard, J.C. (1835). *Treatise on insanity*. London: Gilbert and Piper.

Prins, H. (1993). Anti-social (psychopathic) personality disorders and dangerousness: Two potentially dangerous concepts. In P. Tyrer & G. Stein (eds), *Personality disorder reviewed*. London: Gaskell Books.

Prins, H. (1980). *Offenders, deviants or patients: An introduction to the study of socio-forensic problems*. London: Tavistock.

Prins, H. (1995). *Offenders, deviants or patients?* (2nd ed.). London: Routledge.

Prins, H. (1997). Dangerous obsessions: Some aspects of jealousy and erotomania. *Psychiatric Care*, *4*, 108–13.

Prins, H. (1998). Characteristics of consultant forensic psychiatrists: A modest survey. *Journal of Forensic Psychiatry*, *9*, 139–49.

Reed, J. (1995). Risk assessment and risk management: The lessons from recent inquiries. In J. Braggins & C. Martin (eds), *Managing risk: achieving the possible*. London: Institute for the Study and Treatment of Delinquency.

Roth, Sir M. (1990). Psychopathic (sociopathic) personality. In R. Bluglass & P. Bowden (eds), *Principles and practice of forensic psychiatry*. London: Churchill Livingstone.

Scott, P.D. (1960). The treatment of psychopaths. *British Medical Journal*, *2*, 1641–6.

Scott, P.D. 1964). Approved School success rates. *British Journal of Criminology*, *4*, 525–56.

Scott, P.D. (1975). *Has psychiatry failed the treatment of offenders?* London: Institute for the Study and Treatment of Delinquency.

Selling, L.S. (1940). The psychiatric findings in the cases of 500 traffic offenders and accident-prone drivers. *American Journal of Psychiatry*, *97*, 68–79.

Shipkowensky, N. (1969). Cyclophrenia and murder. In A.V.S. de Rueck & R. Porter (eds), *The mentally abnormal offender*. London: Churchill.

Skett, S., & Stepney, J. (1995). Personality disorders: Research up-date. *Forensic Up-Date*, *43*, 3–12.

Steadman, H., Mulvey, E.P., Monahan, J., Robbins, P.C., Applebaum, P.S., Griso, T., Roth, L.H., & Silver, E. (1998). Violence by people discharged from acute psychiatric in-patient facilities and by others in the same neighbourhoods. *Archives of General Psychiatry*, *55*, 393–401.

Stein, G. (1993). Drug treatment in personality disorders. In P. Tyrer & G. Stein (eds), *Personality disorder reviewed*. London: Gaskell Books.

Swanson, J.W., Holtzer, C.E., Ganju, V.K., & Juno, R.T. (1990). Violence and psychiatric disorder in the community: Evidence from the epidemiologic catchment area surveys. *Hospital and Community Psychiatry*, *41*, 761–70.

Szasz, T. (1987). *Insanity: The idea and its consequences*. New York: Wiley.

Taylor, P.J. (1985). Motives for offending among violent and psychotic men. *British Journal of Psychiatry*, *147*, 491–8.

Taylor, P.J. (1995). Schizophrenia and the risk of violence. In S.R. Hirsch & D.R. Weinberger (eds), *Schizophrenia*. Oxford: Blackwell.

Taylor, P.J., Mahendra, B., & Gunn, J. (1983). Erotomania in males. *Psychological Medicine*, *13*, 645–50.

Taylor, P.J., & Gunn, J. (1984). Violence and psychosis: Risk of violence among psychotic men. *British Medical Journal*, *288*, 1945–9.

Taylor, P.J., Leese, M., Williams, D., Butwell, M., Daly, C., & Larkin, E. (1998). Mental disorder and violence: A Special (high security) Hospital study. *British Journal of Psychiatry*, *172*, 218–16.

Tennent, G., Tennent, D., Prins, H., & Bedford, A. (1980). Psychopathic personality: A useful clinical concept? *Medicine, Science and the Law, 30*, 39–44.

Tennent, G., Tennent, D., Prins, H., & Bedford, A. (1983). Is psychopathic disorder a treatable condition? *Medicine, Science and the Law, 33*, 63–6.

Thompson, C.B. (1937). A psychiatric study of recidivists. *American Journal of Psychiatry, 94*, 591–604.

Treves-Brown, C. (1977). Who is the psychopath? *Medicine, Science and the Law, 17*, 56–73.

Tupin, J.P., Mahar, D., & Smith, D. (1973). Two types of violent offenders with psychosocial descriptors. *Diseases of the Nervous System, 34*, 356–63.

Tyrer, P. (1989). Clinical importance of personality disorder. *Current Opinion in Psychiatry, 2*, 240–3.

Tyrer, P. (1998). Feedback for the personality disordered. *Journal of Forensic Psychiatry, 9*, 1–4.

Tyrer, P., & Stein, G. (eds). (1993). *Personality disorder reviewed*. London: Gaskell Books.

Vetter, H. (1990). Dissociation, psychopathy and the serial murderer. In S. Egger (ed.), *Serial murder: An elusive phenomenon*. London: Praeger.

Wallace, C., Mullen, P., Burgess, P., Palmer, S., Ruschen, A.D., & Browne, C. (1998). Serious criminal offending and mental disorder: A case linkage study. *British Journal of Psychiatry, 172*, 477–84.

Wambaugh, J. (1989). *The blooding*. London: Bantam Books.

Wesseley, S.C., Castle, D., Douglas, A.J., & Taylor, P.J. (1994). The criminal careers of incident cases of schizophrenia. *Psychological Medicine, 24*, 483–502.

Widiger, T.A., & Trull, T.J. (1994). Personality disorders and violence. In J. Monahan & H.J. Steadman (eds), *Violence and mental disorder: Developments in risk assessment*. London and Chicago: University of Chicago Press.

West, D.J. (1963). *The habitual prisoner*. London: Macmillan.

West, D.J. (1965). *Murder followed by suicide*. London: Macmillan.

Wheatley, M. (1998). The prevalence and relevance of substance use in detained schizophrenic patients. *Journal of Forensic Psychiatry, 9*, 114–30.

Whiteley, S.J. (1994). In pursuit of the elusive category. *British Journal of Psychiatry Review of Books, 7*, 14–17.

Winnicott, D.W. (1949). Hate in the countertransference. *International Journal of Psychoanalysis, 30*, 69–74.

Woddis, G.M. (1964). Clinical psychiatry and crime. *British Journal of Criminology, 4*, 443–60.

Wootton, B. (1959). *Social science and social pathology*. London: Allen and Unwin.

World Health Organisation. (1992). *Classification of mental and behavioural disorders: Clinical descriptions and diagnostic guidelines*. Geneva: Author (WHO).

Chapter 4

With the (doubtful) benefit of hindsight

Risk assessment carried out through rose-tinted glasses can be fatal.
Sir Louis Blom-Cooper, 1995

Despite the considerable extent of media hype and political sensitivities referred to earlier in this book, there have been a number of occasions where procedures and practices relating to the care and management of offenders and offender–patients in the community have been found to be unsatisfactory. Such concerns, for example, led to the setting up in 1994 of mandatory independent inquiries into all those cases where homicides had been committed by those in contact with the mental health services. In other cases (such as homicides committed by those being managed by non-mental health services) there is no mandatory provision for an inquiry, but an internal investigation will normally be held. In this chapter, I have selected a number of inquiries for comment; a word or two of explanation is necessary concerning the somewhat arbitrary manner in which they have been chosen.

With two exceptions they are all inquiries into homicide. The two exceptions are first, the inquiry I chaired into the death in seclusion of Orville Blackwood in Broadmoor Hospital; the second (which I also chaired) was into the abscsonion of an offender–patient from an escorted day trip to a theme park with a zoo. I have chosen to include these two, partly because they illustrate some aspects of risk-taking practices not always found in some homicide inquiries, and partly because I was involved in them personally. The remaining inquiries I have chosen all concern homicides committed by persons known to the psychiatric services; and a number of them were set up before 1994, when such inquiries became mandatory. Some aspects of the ground I cover have also been dealt with by others; notably Reith's recent comprehensive review of twenty-eight homicide and other inquiries about people known to mental health services between 1988 and 1997 (Reith, 1998a; 1998b). Summaries of inquiry reports for a more extended period (1969–94) have been provided by Sheppard (1996). (For subsequent up-dates see Zito Trust, 1997a; 1997b; 1998a & 1998b). My intention is to draw attention to certain criticisms made in these various reports which will serve as a springboard for a consideration in Chapter 5 of how practice might be improved.

Inquiries into serious incidents (including deaths) are not new phenomena in the UK. In the 1960s, there were numerous inquiries into the abuse of patients in psychiatric hospitals and in institutions providing geriatric care; from the 1970s onwards we have seen an escalation of inquiries into child abuse of various kinds, particularly those which have investigated the abuse of children by professional carers. With regard to mental health inquiries more specifically, the focus has moved from inquiries into institutional care to inquiries into care in community settings. Two policy developments have taken place. The first has been the introduction of the *National confidential inquiry into homicides and suicides by mentally ill people* by the Department of Health with the co-operation of the Royal College of Psychiatrists. The objectives are to inquire into and collect overall data on homicides and suicides committed by people under the care of, or recently discharged into, the community, by mental health services. The Steering Committee which had been set up to carry out this work made a preliminary report in 1994 and a full report in 1996 (Steering Committee, 1994; 1996). Recommendations flowing from both reports included the need for improved assessment techniques, better contact with patients, better communication between professionals and better liaison between psychiatric professionals and those in close contact with the family carers of patients. (These matters will be the subject of further comment when individual inquiry reports are examined.) The inquiry (now named the *National confidential inquiry into suicide and homicide by people with mental illness*) has been relocated at the University of Manchester. (Appleby et al., 1997). It will continue to collect and collate data, but using a more refined approach. It will not be concerned with making inquiries into individual cases. These inquiries are the subject of different procedures to be outlined in detail later.

The description and discussion of these inquiries takes the following form: *first*, an account of what I shall call more general inquiries where risk elements appeared to be important; *second*, a selection of inquiries that predated the 1994 Department of Health instruction for mandatory independent inquiries; and *third*, an account of certain inquiries subsequent to that instruction.[1]

The Sharon Campbell inquiry

Sharon Campbell, a patient with a history of mental illness, stabbed to death her former social worker, Isabel Schwarz. This followed an assault some months earlier and alleged threats by Sharon Campbell. She was found guilty of manslaughter on the grounds of diminished responsibility and made the subject of a Hospital Order with restrictions under Sections 37/41 of the Mental Health Act 1983. One of the key factors emerging from the inquiry into her care was a history of poor compliance with medication. In addition, her willingness to accept social work support and supervision was very variable. The inquiry, chaired by John Spokes, QC, indicated that although mental health resources were available they were not being used very effectively. The inquiry team was impressed with the effort and time being put into the case by many different professionals, but in the months leading up to the attack there had been a dearth of psychiatric treatment and close and regular supervision. It is of interest to note that although the killing of Miss Schwarz took place in 1984, the inquiry report only appeared three years later, in 1988 – a considerable delay. The report had a great deal to say about the need for employing authorities to set in place procedures that would maximise the personal safety of social work and allied staff (Spokes, 1988).

The Graham Young inquiry

Graham Young was sent to Broadmoor in 1962 under Sections 60 and 65 of the Mental Health Act 1959, having been convicted of administering poison to his father. There are allegations that he had also poisoned his stepmother over a long period of time through the administration of antimony, finally killing her through the administration of thallium. Some eight years after his admission to Broadmoor he was conditionally discharged on the recommendation of his Responsible Medical Officer. He was found work in a warehouse at a photographic development company at Bovingdon in Hertfordshire, and was found lodgings. He was supervised by a psychiatrist and a local probation officer. In the light of subsequent events, it is of interest to note that before discharge from Broadmoor he had applied for two posts – one at a forensic science laboratory, and another at a pharmaceutical training school. Within three months of his discharge Young had poisoned three of his workmates with thallium which he obtained from a firm of leading dispensing chemists in central London. Suspicion fairly quickly fell on Young and he was subsequently charged and brought to trial. He pleaded not guilty to murder (on the basis that he wanted maximum publicity for his activities). He was sentenced to life imprisonment on two charges of murder and two of attempted murder. Following the sentence, two inquiries were established: the first into the specifics of Young's case (Aarvold et al., 1973, the Aarvold inquiry); the second, a more wide-ranging inquiry into the management of mentally disordered offenders within the criminal justice system (HO & DHSS, 1975, The Butler Committee). The Aarvold inquiry made a number of important recommendations concerning the supervision of restricted offender–patients and the over-ready availability of poisons for purchase by members of the public. As a result of the inquiry a permanent body was established to advise the Home Secretary on restricted cases requiring special care in assessment (Home Secretary's Advisory Board).

A number of important questions emerged from the Aarvold Report: first, whether adequate attention prior to discharge was paid to Young's long-standing obsessive preoccupation with poisons; second, how much was known about his two employment applications before discharge; third, the wisdom of allowing him to take up employment in an industry where he could have ready access to poisonous substances; and fourth, questions arise about the adequacy of supervision by his supervisors (to be fair to the probation service, they claim they were not given adequate information about Young's past history); it has been suggested that he was never visited in his lodgings. When the police went there following his arrest, they found a variety of chemicals and bizarre drawings of men in varying stages of dying, including some pictures of them with hair loss – a feature of thallium poisoning.

Some three years or so after his life sentence, Young developed a mental illness serious enough to warrant formal transfer back into the Special Hospital system under the Mental Health Act 1983. However, it was felt subsequently that he should be returned to prison. Bowden (1996: 23) quotes the telling conclusions at a case conference held at Park Lane Special Hospital in June, 1982:

We can do little else but recommend that Graham be returned to whence he came and repay his debt to society and his victims in the normal way.

And so it was to be. In August 1990, this complex man died in Parkhurst Prison aged 42 from natural causes (heart attack).[2]

The shootings at Dunblane Primary School

In the early morning of 13 March 1996 Thomas Hamilton approached the car park at Dunblane Primary School where he proceeded to cut the telephone wires which served some neighbouring houses. He then entered the school armed with four handguns and 743 rounds of ammunition. He went into the Assembly Hall and began firing; subsequently he went into other adjacent parts of the school, firing indiscriminately. Hamilton eventually turned his weapon on himself placing a revolver in his mouth and died shortly afterwards. As a result of this mass carnage sixteen children and one member of staff died. Hamilton inflicted gunshot wounds on ten other pupils and three other members of the teaching staff. In what must be one of the most detailed and measured reports of its kind, Lord Cullen (1996: 2) outlines some of the background factors which might have been in Hamilton's mind on that fateful day.

> His [Boys'] clubs were in decline. He was in serious financial difficulties. His mood was low and he was deeply resentful of those who had claimed he was a pervert and had discouraged boys from attending his clubs. After a gap of about eight years his interest in firearms was resurgent. There is evidence which points to his making preparations for what he did ... in the light of expert evidence from a psychologist and psychiatrist, I conclude that Thomas Hamilton was not mentally ill but had a paranoid personality with a desire to control others in which his firearms were the focus of his fantasies. The violence which he used would not have been predictable. His previous conduct showed indications of paedophilia.

At various times Hamilton's fitness to possess firearms should have been questioned more closely. For example, in 1989 his authority to possess firearms and ammunition was not questioned after he had 'behaved inappropriately in showing firearms to a family in Linlithgow'. In 1991, a detective sergeant in a formal memorandum challenged his fitness to be trusted with a firearm. This followed a police investigation of certain events at a summer camp run by Hamilton. Lord Cullen is highly critical of the lack of follow-up of this memorandum. He says 'on balance, there was a case for revocation which should have been acted upon. The same considerations should have led in any event to the refusal of Thomas Hamilton's subsequent applications for renewal of his firearm certificate' (p. 2). One has the impression that because the detective sergeant's position was not a very high one in the constabulary hierarchy it was probably not given the serious consideration it should have been. A similar situation arose in the case of Jason Mitchell which I discuss subsequently. The hierarchical nature of many mental health and criminal justice organisations sometimes seems to militate against adequate consideration of important pieces of information or expression of opinion by those who are not regarded as having significant roles to play.

The case of Daniel Mudd

Daniel Mudd had been released in 1983 on conditional discharge from Broadmoor, where he had been originally detained for non-homicide offences (arson and assault). In 1986, during his period of supervision in the community, he killed a fellow (female) resident in a mental aftercare hostel; he was subsequently sentenced to life imprisonment. An internal committee of inquiry was established (Wiltshire County Council, 1988); their findings revealed what appear to have been a number of serious errors of judgement and practice. These are summarised as follows:

1   Too little attention had been paid to the nature of Mudd's previous offences, behaviour and convictions prior to hospitalisation; these had included making indecent phone calls, assault with intent to commit actual bodily harm, and indecent assault on an adult female.
2   Too little attention appeared to have been paid to the views of the doctors who examined him at his trial; they said he was potentially very dangerous and, because of the nature of his particular personality disorder, might well kill someone at some future date.
3   Although this young man had been in the care of the local authority concerned with his current supervision for many years, no attempt appeared to have been made to collate the data in the numerous files about him that were available, and would have provided an extended personality profile. In addition (and very unwisely in my view) no-one had thought it useful to consult the social worker who had known and supervised him as a youngster.
4   Mudd had very serious drinking problems during the period of supervision. These, it was alleged, had never been properly identified or placed in the context of his past behaviour and attitudes.

There were said to have been occasions when he was so affected by drink that he could not get up to go to work.

5   This lack of identification continued, even when he was picked up on several occasions by the police for being drunk and when he had assaulted a man whilst under the influence of drink. He had also been discharged prematurely from a training scheme because of alleged sexual advances to a woman trainee.

6   His supervising social worker left and no attempt appeared to have been made to prepare Mudd for his departure. It was also alleged that he was left unsupervised for a month.

7   The Committee of Inquiry found that throughout the period of supervision Mudd's version of events had been accepted at face value and without challenge. The records available (which were in any case difficult to interpret) showed no indications of any critical analysis of events and attitudes. Supervision by senior management had not been effective. The supervisors seemed to have adopted a preconceived notion that Mudd was someone who needed to be 'rescued' from an adverse life experience (that is, having been detained in a Special Hospital) and that this preoccupation had blinded them to the realities of the case. Finally, it was felt that the supervisors took too much upon themselves and did not liaise sufficiently well with the relevant Home Office department; in addition, they had failed to provide that department with adequate information about the progress of the case.

The Allitt inquiry

During the period February to April, 1991, there was a series of unexpected and unexplained events on the children's ward at Grantham and Kesteven General Hospital. 'Three children died suddenly on the ward, and a baby died at home not long after discharge' (Clothier et al., 1994: 5). Following further medical 'emergencies' on the ward, a suspicion developed that someone was deliberately harming the child victims. A lengthy police investigation followed and eventually an enrolled nurse, Beverly Allitt, was charged with four murders, nine attempted murders and nine counts of causing grievous bodily harm with intent to the same children. She was also charged with attempting to murder two adults outside the hospital and causing them grievous bodily harm with intent. She was sentenced to life imprisonment on every count, but found not guilty of the charges concerning the two adults. Following sentence she was readmitted to a Special Hospital where she had been detained before her trial. Following Allitt's conviction and sentence an urgent inquiry was set up into what was rightly regarded as a series of shocking events within an NHS hospital.

The inquiry was searching and very thorough. Summarising their main conclusions, Sir Cecil Clothier (1994) and his colleagues point to the main failures 'which contributed to vulnerability, to outrage, or incapacity to contain it' (p. 125). These were: (i) sloppy investigation of Allitt's background employment and the significance of her health record (for example, repeated absences due to alleged sickness); (ii) inadequate levels of nursing staff on the ward in question and lack of leadership and positive action by senior ward management; (iii) laxity of operational procedures by senior management; (iv) lack of prompt response by senior consultant staff to so many collapses by the child patients in their care. The inquiry team contended that 'if a meeting involving staff in all disciplines had been convened, as it should have been as soon as the chance determination of events began to strain credulity, there is a strong likelihood that their malevolent cause would have been detected' (p. 126); (v) a failure to act on a request for a *post mortem* on the first victim to be carried out by a specialist paediatric pathologist. This might have averted the subsequent sad train of events; and (vi) ineptness of responses to the grossly abnormal insulin levels in one of the children and a lack of recognition of abnormalities in the chest x-rays in two of the children who survived Allitt's attacks.

In concluding their list of criticisms the inquiry team had this to say:

> We have identified what we see as the main failures and objects of criticism in this grievous story. They vary in significance in terms of their contribution to the delay in bringing it to an end. No single circumstance or individual can be held responsible for what happened. *But taken together* [emphasis added], the catalogue of lapses from high standards to which the National Health Service aspires point to lessons which should be heeded if every effort is to be made to contain such a catastrophe should it strike again.
>
> (Clothier et al., 1994: 128)

In an epilogue to the report, the inquiry team make two other insightful and sensitive observations – observations that could usefully be heeded by all those charged with inquiries into serious incidents:

> Where we have found culpability, we believe we have placed it firmly where it belongs. But those whom we have criticised were

subjected by chance to a test more severe than any which most of us encounter in a lifetime: so we have not striven to find fault merely to satisfy a popular urge to see suffering in others as the proper response to one's own . . .

We were struck throughout our Inquiry by the way in which fragments of medical evidence which, if assembled, would have pointed to Allitt as the malevolent cause of the unexpected collapses of children, lay neglected or were missed altogether. Taken in isolation, these fragments of medical evidence were not all very significant nor was the failure to recognise some of them very culpable. But collectively they would have amounted to an unmistakable portrait of malevolence. The principal failure of those concerned lay in not collecting together those pieces of evidence.

(Clothier et al., 1994: 131)

THREE SOMEWHAT DIFFERENT BUT RELEVANT INQUIRIES

The death of Orville Blackwood

In September, 1991, the Special Hospitals Service Authority, as it then was, set up an inquiry under my chairmanship to investigate the death of a young African-Caribbean patient, Orville Blackwood and, at the same time, to review the reports of previous inquiries into two other deaths of African-Caribbean patients in Broadmoor, Michael Martin and Joseph Watts, in order to see if there were any common themes (Prins et al., 1993). The inquiry was not established to investigate individual complaints: we were examining patterns of practice within the hospital which might have contributed to the deaths of the three patients.

Orville, a large man, had a record of being in trouble with the police from an early age; by the time he was in his twenties he had spent short periods in prison. At the age of 22 he developed a remitting and relapsing psychotic illness, and in the next two years or so had a number of admissions (some compulsory) to psychiatric hospitals. During this period he was diagnosed as suffering from a variety of illnesses, including acute paranoid state and drug-induced psychosis. Early in 1986, Orville was arrested for robbing a bookmaker's shop with a toy gun. Because no bed was available in the local Regional Secure Unit (RSU) he was sentenced to three years' imprisonment. However, a year into his sentence, his mental state deteriorated to the extent that he was transferred to an RSU. Following a period of acute disturbance, during which he seriously assaulted a nurse, he was transferred to Broadmoor. He presented considerable management problems and became increasingly disturbed. Early in August 1991, his periods of disturbance seemed to become more frequent and serious; on 18 August, following an altercation with the staff, he was secluded. Subsequently, he was forcibly medicated and left in seclusion. Shortly after this he was observed to have stopped breathing. Resuscitation proved unsuccessful and Orville was found to be dead on arrival at the local general hospital.

During our inquiry we met on nineteen occasions to hear oral evidence from some fifty witnesses; we also met on seven occasions to formulate and finalise our report. Various problems beset us at the outset; an initial reluctance on the part of the national Prison Officers' Association to allow their members at Broadmoor to participate in the inquiry (subsequently overcome); and demands from all sides to conduct our inquiry in public and to concentrate on particular issues. We reached a wide range of conclusions at the end of our investigation (making 47 recommendations which occupied 5 pages of our 87-page report). I have selected one or two that seem particularly relevant to the matters under discussion in this book. First, we thought there had been something of a knee-jerk reaction to Orville's behaviour; notably on the fatal morning when he had refused to go to occupational therapy. Instead of offering a discussion of what might have been his reasons for not wishing to go, seclusion and medication were the subsequent responses. Throughout his stay in Broadmoor there seemed to be a tendency not to discriminate between his illness-driven conduct and that for which there was a quite rational explanation; namely his concerns about his length of stay in hospital and the way in which he felt he and his fellow African-Caribbean patients were being discriminated against. We considered that, during his stay, his treatment as a black patient did not seem to be very sensitive and that his 'dangerousness' had been stressed unduly to the point that it obscured consideration of other important elements in his life. We had no doubt that a culture of racism existed in Broadmoor, most of it at a level of institutional racial bias against ethnic minorities. Such institutional bias has recently come to the fore again as a result of the findings of the public inquiry into Stephen Lawrence's murder and the subsequent police investigation of his killing (Macpherson, 1999). An article in the *Independent* of 3 August 1998 reporting on recent and highly relevant research into racist attitudes in the Metropolitan Police led me to write the following letter which was published in that paper four days later:

Rooted Racism

Sir: Although highly disturbing, Dr. Oakley's findings of institutional racism in the Metropolitan Police ('Police accused of "racist culture"', 3 August) will come as no surprise to those of us whose explorations of racism take them into institutional settings, be they open or closed. I chaired the independent inquiry into the death of Orville Blackwood in Broadmoor Hospital in 1993. He was a young Afro-Caribbean offender–patient with a history of schizophrenic illness. Two earlier reports into the deaths of two other Afro-Caribbean patients, which we were asked to re-evaluate, had found no direct evidence of racism in Broadmoor and many of the witnesses at our inquiry did not believe that this was a problem in the hospital. However, we were of the firm opinion that such views were 'based on an interpretation of racism founded on very crude measures' and that the staff and management just did not recognise the subtle ways in which racism could operate. We concluded that there was racism in Broadmoor, but not on the whole deliberate or necessarily conscious; rather it was an extreme lack of sensitivity to the needs and cultural differences of ethnic minority patients. Of our 47 recommendations, several were directed at ethnic issues. These included the need to appoint black staff at senior management level and to have black representation on the managing health authority. We also offered to return to the hospital to monitor the implementation of our recommendations – an offer firmly declined at that time. Somewhat ironically, a few weeks ago, I was asked to return to Broadmoor to participate in a seminar examining how successful the hospital had been in developing its anti-racist policies and practices! I learnt that there were still no black members of senior management, neither was there any black representation on the managing health authority. It also appeared that there were even fewer black staff working on the wards than at the time of our inquiry. All institutions are notoriously impervious to change; the only way to bring about such change is to make them more openly accountable. Sadly, we still have a long way to go.
HERSCHEL PRINS

(*Independent*, 7 August 1998, p. 2)

Ethnic bias is a vitally important element in making assessments of risk and its subsequent management. There is still a very real need for criminal justice and mental health professionals to recognise the extent to which their prejudices may be operating at subliminal levels of consciousness.

Area Child Protection Committee's review in respect of Charmaine and Heather West[3]

Area Child Protection Committees (ACPCs) are required to carry out what is known as a Part 8 review of a case either where a child dies as a result of abuse or neglect, or it is in the public interest to do so. Following the trial and sentencing of Rosemary West, Gloucestershire Social Services Department published a report by the Bridge Child Care Consultancy Service (on behalf of eight other agencies involved in the past care of the two West children, Charmaine and Heather). Charmaine died in about 1971 and Heather probably in 1987. The Bridge Child Care Consultancy Service (1995) *Review Report* covers a period of 36 years. One of the important factors emerging from the *Review* was the wide disparity apparent concerning the retention of past records by the various agencies involved. Another important point to emerge was the need to maintain long-term chronologies detailing key events. These examined as a whole and over time often convey a greater degree of significance than when seen in isolation (cf. the inquiry findings in the Allitt case above and the Robinson case below). For example, the Consultancy identified clusters of events like numerous referrals to Hospital Accident and Emergency (A and E) Departments and other agencies which might have alerted some of them to the fact that all was not well in the family. The Consultancy makes a compelling observation: 'At the time the conditions were presented to the A and E and other departments they were being seen in isolation and the information recorded in different file records thus preventing the possibility of detecting anything untoward' (p. 9; cf. the findings of the inquiry team in the case of Daniel Mudd referred to above). However, although making this critical comment, the Consultancy state that 'none of the information could be said to indicate the presence of potential multiple murders' (p. 9). The light sentences handed out to Fred and Rosemary West for offences involving indecency in the early 1970s gave the team cause to make the following trenchant observation:

> It may be that the apparent light, non-custodial sentences confused the way in which risk to the children was perceived, if it was considered at all. Certainly, looking back, it is puzzling as to how

custodial sentences 20+ years ago were handed out to Frederick West for non payment of fines, but not for a conviction for indecent assault and causing bodily harm.

(Bridge Child Care Consultancy Service, 1995: 11)

The inquiry also raises the vital issue of listening to what children are trying to tell various officials, thus:

Given that some of the children in the West family had talked of a family joke involving Heather being under the patio, it would appear that someone managed to enforce a way of living that kept the children out of reach of the child protection services (p. 11).

However, by August 1993, Social Services were becoming concerned at *repeated comments* [emphasis added] by some of the children about Heather being under the patio. A decision was taken to pass the information to the police and the subsequent investigation resulted in a not untypical child protection case turning into a search which led to the finding of 12 murder victims (p. 13).

Finally, the Consultancy *Report* had this to say about listening to children in particular:

The social work staff, lawyers and police who listened to the West children, evaluated their comments and acted, should be commended for their ability to respond objectively and for their willingness to risk their professional reputations on the basis of what they were being told. It would have been so easy to do nothing rather than take the risk because the comments of the children appeared bizarre. The actions of those who listened to the West children have provided a salutary lesson to all professionals working in child protection, whether social workers, teachers, doctors, lawyers, police or the judiciary, not to dismiss lightly the comments of children however bizarre (pp. 19–20).

Such comments can, of course, be applied with equal force to the 'stories' told by adults.

The manner in which courts deal with offenders following current convictions, the relevance of previous convictions and the need to listen to what witnesses (particularly children) are trying to impart, are matters that are explored further in the final chapter.

Absconsion of an offender–patient from a medium secure unit

Mr H. was an offender–patient in his fifties who had a long history of institutional care, alcohol abuse and a substantial record of criminal convictions for a variety of offences, which had led to periods of both imprisonment and hospitalisation. Many of these offences were of a relatively minor nature; however, over the years he was convicted of sex offences and physical assault. His first sexually motivated offence was in 1985, when he was convicted of Assault Occasioning Actual Bodily Harm for striking a 14-year-old boy who rejected his sexual advances. Subsequently, he had convictions for indecency and attempting to procure acts of gross indecency, his sexual interest being directed particularly towards boys aged 15–16. However, some of his victims had been in the 10–12 years age range. In 1988 he was convicted of Assault Occasioning Actual Bodily Harm and received a five-year prison sentence. Over the years he had persistently written obscene and threatening letters and sent obscene publications through the post. He had also sent abusive and threatening letters to various persons involved in his care and management. In 1992 he was admitted to St. Andrew's Hospital, Northampton, under Section 37 of the Mental Health Act 1983, following a conviction for indecency and attempting to procure gross indecency. Despite making some progress at St. Andrew's Hospital, he was discharged in 1994 on the grounds that he no longer fulfilled the treatability criteria of the Act. Shortly after discharge, he was arrested and subsequently convicted of indecency with a child under 14 years and for sending obscene materials by post; he received a sentence of three years' imprisonment.

Released in 1995, he was quickly in trouble again for sending malicious letters by post and assault on a police officer. Following delays occasioned by difficulties in finding suitable mental health care for him, he was admitted to a Medium Secure Unit in May 1996, and subsequently made subject to a further Hospital Order under Section 37 of the Mental Health Act in June. His progress in the unit was not satisfactory; in addition to episodes of violence and abuse to staff, he succeeded in a determined effort to abscond, remaining free for twelve hours. However, there was no evidence available to the inquiry panel that he did anything unlawful during this period. Throughout his stay in the secure unit he showed himself to be unco-operative and unwilling to involve himself fully in assessment procedures. However, his lack of co-operation might have been better understood if more detailed information about his background and past testing of his intellectual functioning had been sought by the unit. Despite his lack of co-operation and his abusive behaviour, he was granted escorted leave outwith the unit. This was because the unit policy did not view leave as an incentive or a reward, but was seen as an important therapeutic intervention. In his case, the RMO and nursing staff said he was granted leave because he was constantly complaining about his lack of freedom and the severe level of restrictions for what he considered to have been a trivial offence. (His admission under the Hospital Order had been made upon conviction for sending malicious letters and for a non-sexual assault following a fracas in a public house.)

His first period of escorted leave occurred only three weeks after his admission to the unit. Following this, he had some thirty escorted leaves for both recreational and non-recreational purposes – all of which passed without incident. Two of these trips were to a nearby zoo. In the inquiry panel's view this seemed not only premature but hazardous in the light of his previous criminal behaviour and openly admitted preference for teenage boys. It is important to state here that we were told 'it is not part of the Unit's policy to take sex offenders to places frequented by children in order to test out their reactions . . . [such] trips were entirely of a recreational nature' (Prins et al., 1997: 18). It was agreed that Mr H. should be taken on an escorted visit to Chessington Zoo and Theme Park (Chessington World of Adventures). Shortly before the trip was due to take place it was discovered that the zoo and the theme park had a common entrance. Despite this, it was agreed that the trip should proceed but 'be restricted to the area where the animals were mainly located' (p. 19). The visit took place with only one nurse escort (his very recently allocated named nurse). Unknown to his escort, the patient had nearer £100.00 on him rather than the £45.00 that had been allocated to him for the trip. Our inquiries revealed that he had a long-standing history of finding ways of accumulating monies without the knowledge of staff. In the event, they did not visit the zoo, but went to the adjacent pub and restaurant. During this period the patient went to the toilet several times; although having checked the position of the toilets in the pub, his escorting nurse failed to spot that there was an alternative exit from the gents' past the entrance to the female toilet. The location of this alternative exit would have been very difficult for a single nurse escort to detect. On the third occasion when the patient visited the toilet he left his jacket with his nurse escort, *but took his wallet with him*. Because he was there a long time (about eight minutes) his escort went into the toilet and enquired whether he was all right. He received an affirmative response. They were about to leave the toilet when the patient announced he needed to go again. Shortly afterwards the nurse escort saw him leave and make his escape via the exit past the female toilet. Despite an intensive search he was not apprehended until some two days later (in Sussex), having been identified by a member of the public. So far as we were able to ascertain, there were no unlawful incidents during this second period of absconsion. We were particularly concerned to learn that the day before he absconded, the patient had handed a sealed letter (addressed personally to his RMO) to a clinical team manager in which 'he clearly threatened to abscond and indicated where he intended to go' (p. 20). The RMO informed us that he did not receive this until after the event. I think our comments concerning the granting of leave and the absconsion are worth quoting at some length.

> Whilst we understand that transport arrangements need to be flexible [due to a shortage of staff a nurse manager drove the patient and his escort to Chessington and then returned to the unit], the arrangements for the trip to Chessington were such as to place the escorting nurse and the patient in a position of some vulnerability, effectively stranded without means of transport, far from the base unit without means of transport and with few options available should anything go wrong. Leave was granted specifically to visit Chessington Zoo and not the Theme Park. The staff should have known more about the disposition of the venue before leave was granted . . . in general we feel there needs to be a more careful evaluation of staffing and other resources required for every escorted trip in relation to both the patient and the chosen venue. In the absence of a specific policy for dealing with absconsions outwith the Unit, it is the Panel's view that the actions taken by the named nurse were appropriate in the circumstances.
>
> (Prins et al., 1997: 21)

As a result of our inquiry we found a number of serious deficiencies concerning risk assessment. For example, there was no systematic procedure in place for recording risk assessment and management and one would have to hunt through the patient's case notes to find the various elements of these assessments. In more specific terms we found as follows:

> The decision to grant leave to the patient so early after his admission seemed to the Panel to be ill-judged and displayed a degree of

therapeutic over-optimism in the face of clear evidence to the contrary. His first leave was granted only five weeks after he had made a determined, if opportunistic absconsion . . . his assessment was incomplete and he was persistently failing to co-operate with this and with treatment. He continued to present substantial behavioural difficulties in the Unit and was attempting to make unauthorised phone calls to his victims and to send obscene and abusive letters. A number of [our] witnesses and other criminal justice and mental health professionals considered him to be a potential danger because of his impulsive aggression, use of alcohol, and his sexual offences against teenage boys. The following list of risk factors should have been considered:

(a)   His substantial criminal history including a charge of wounding;
(b)   His escalating criminal behaviour;
(c)   His sex offences – their nature, his lack of insight, lack of remorse and blatant disagreement with the law relating to consent;
(d)   His threatening letters, some of which threatened to kill and physically harm;
(e)   The relationship between his use of alcohol and his aggressive behaviour;
(f)   His low frustration tolerance as evidenced by his behaviour when thwarted;
(g)   His persistent failure to co-operate with assessment and treatment;
(h)   His age and previous long history and failure to respond to treatment;
(i)   The concerns expressed [to us] by the police and other professionals;
(j)   His recurring threats to abscond and his previous absconsion.

(Prins et al., 1997: 25)

Taken together, these elements reveal what would appear to be a singularly over-optimistic view of the patient's risk potential; and amply illustrates the quotation at the heading of this chapter.

SOME MENTAL HEALTH HOMICIDE INQUIRIES PRIOR TO 1994

The inquiry into the care and management of Sharon Campbell was the first into mental health care provisions for patients who have committed homicide. Those that now follow are of inquiries initiated prior to the 1994 Department of Health instructions.

Carol Barratt

Carol Barratt was a young woman with a long history of psychiatric difficulties. Two days after her discharge from the Psychiatric Unit of Doncaster Royal Infirmary, she stabbed to death an 11-year-old girl in a shopping mall. Prior to this event, she had been detained under Section 2 of the Mental Health Act 1983, following an incident during which she had threatened with a knife a young woman in the same shopping area. During her detention under Section 2, she applied to a Mental Health Review Tribunal for her discharge. The Tribunal did not discharge, taking the view that 'She needs supervision at the present time and should not be discharged from the Section' (see Unwin et al., 1991). Following representations made by her mother, Barratt's RMO discharged her. The RMO was criticised in the inquiry report for making 'a serious error of clinical judgement'. The *Committee of inquiry* also made a number of recommendations concerning nursing care and practices (Unwin et al., 1991).

Kim Kirkman

Kim Kirkman was charged with the murder of a neighbour, but before he could come to trial he committed suicide whilst on remand. He had previously been detained for some seventeen years under the provisions of both the 1959 and 1983 Mental Health Acts following a history of serious non-homicide offences. He made significantly good progress for him to be granted a deferred conditional discharge by the Home Office. However, within a day of this being put into effect his neighbour was found murdered. Although the inquiry admitted there was no way in which Kirkman's alleged homicidal behaviour could have been predicted, they did recommend that more use might be made by practitioners of research findings and actuarial devices (Dick et al., 1991).[4]

Christopher Clunis

The inquiry into the care and treatment of Christopher Clunis is possibly the most well known of all mental health homicide inquiries. It has served as a pattern for later inquiry procedures and practices. It was also of importance in paving the way for the introduction of detailed guidance on the care and management of mentally disordered persons with a proclivity for violence. Additionally, it heralded the introduction of 'risk registers' for such individuals. Clunis, a diagnosed schizophrenic, stabbed to death a complete stranger – the recently married Jonathan Zito – on a London Underground railway platform. Following conviction and sentence by way of a Hospital Order with Restrictions (Sections 37 and 41, Mental Health Act 1983), the two Health Authorities concerned with his care and treatment set up an independent inquiry (Ritchie et al., 1994). Their very full and careful account traces the care (and sometimes the lack of it) of Clunis for the period 1986–92. Although the inquiry team singled out a few instances of dedicated care and concern on the part of one or two workers, none of the various agencies concerned escaped serious criticism; for example, the Police, Crown Prosecution, Health and Social Services, the Probation Service and Voluntary Agencies. What emerged overall was not a picture of wilful or intentional neglect of duty, but a failure to spot vital behavioural cues and clues, *and a failure to communicate between agencies at every level*. Had information from a variety of sources been linked, certain deficiencies observed by the inquiry team would have been obviated. Some examples were: (i) failure to obtain a detailed and sequential history of the pattern of Clunis's life style (cf. the cases of Daniel Mudd and the West children above); (ii) failure to consider his past record of violence and to treat it seriously enough to proceed with *prosecution* rather than *diversion* from the criminal justice system; (iii) failure to act assertively enough in dealing with the steady deterioration of his mental condition. They suggest that this failure may have arisen because of an erroneous ideological assumption about not wishing to label Clunis as a schizophrenic in order to avoid stigmatising him; (iv) failure to monitor his progress in pro-active fashion; and (v) inadequate training for mental health and criminal justice professions in this area of work.[5]

Michael Buchanan

Michael Buchanan had a long history of both residential childcare and psychiatric treatment; in his adult years he had numerous brushes with the law. In September 1992, he beat to death a complete stranger (a retired police officer) in an underground car park. His psychiatric history was one of relapsing psychotic illness exacerbated by addiction to cannabis and cocaine. His career in the community was marked by lack of adequate care planning and follow up. The panel of inquiry set up to examine his care recommended that, in order to facilitate better implementation of the Care Programme Approach, representatives from all disciplines and agencies involved in the patient's case should be present at Section 117 Mental Health Act planning meetings. The patient's key worker should *always* be present. Section 117 meetings should have special regard in formulating discharge plans to what was known about the patient's capacity to harm others. The panel also recommended that as far as humanly possible, only experienced staff should be allocated to problematic cases such as Buchanan's (Heginbotham et al., 1994).

Andrew Robinson

Robinson's case has already been referred to in some detail in Chapter 2 when some of the legal and administrative aspects of risk assessment and management were being considered. Another aspect of his case is worth referring to here, with reference to the special concerns of this chapter. This relates to the manner in which the concerns of his parents were not heeded by some of the professionals engaged in his care. At the inquiry they maintained that his outbursts of violence and aggression (due to his recurrent psychotic episodes) had made their home a place of terror. Similar concerns by relatives have been expressed at other homicide inquiries and are referred to shortly.

Jason Mitchell

Mitchell's case was also considered in Chapter 2, for similar reasons. However, there is a rather more clinical aspect to be considered at this point. The inquiry team made a very important observation concerning the need to pay attention to information gathered from a patient from whatever source. Mitchell had a fairly prolonged period of contact with an occupational therapy assistant (OTA) during one of his periods of hospitalisation. During this contact he revealed a great deal of information about his violent thoughts and fantasies which could have provided vital clues to his subsequent conduct. Sadly, this material, which was recorded very systematically by the OTA, appears to have been afforded little if any attention, largely because she was seen as unqualified, and therefore her information was deemed not to be of great note. It should also be noted that the inquiry panel found that her work was largely unsupervised, that she felt out of her depth and at a loss to know what to do with the information she obtained. It seems very important to recognise that the hierarchical nature of criminal justice and mental health care agencies sometimes serves to limit the contributions of those at relatively lower levels in the hierarchy (Blom-Cooper et al., 1996).

Reith cites the example of the inquiry into the care of Raymond Sinclair as providing a similar example. In this case, the clinical team did not regard Sinclair's condition as 'serious or threatening, despite a contrary view expressed by the community psychiatric nurse (CPN), thus undermining the confidence in her own judgement of the relatively inexperienced and unsupervised CPN' (Reith, 1998a; see also Lingham et al., 1996). The case of Richard Burton provides a somewhat similar lesson. Burton killed his landlady following the break-up of a long-term relationship with a girl friend and his self-referral for renewed psychiatric help. Some years previously, he had revealed to a student nurse that he had fantasies of harming his parents and that he had had other violent fantasies since very early adulthood. The information does not appear to have been fed back to senior medical staff (Chapman et al., 1996).

I now consider briefly a number of other inquiries which were set up as a direct consequence of the NHS Executive Guidance on Homicide Inquiries (HSG (94) 27, 10 May 1994). As we will see, a number of them make particular recommendations as to the role of relatives and their needs in work with psychiatric patients/offender–patients.

The Woodley team report

In this report the perpetrator of the homicide (of Dominican background) is referred to only by his initials, SL. In July 1994 SL killed SB, a fellow patient at a Social Services day centre. SL was subsequently ordered to be detained under a Hospital Order with Restrictions (Sections 37 & 41, Mental Health Act 1983) following a plea of guilty to manslaughter on the grounds of diminished responsibility. SL had a long history of penal and hospital care and being diagnosed as a paranoid schizophrenic. The report, which was very comprehensive, makes a number of very important recommendations, only one or two of which are highlighted here. *First* the team is unequivocal in its view that, instead of being afforded a four-year prison sentence, he should have been afforded a hospital disposal (Woodley et al., 1995; 1 & 31). *Second* although the inquiry team commended the efforts made by both SL's probation officer and the social worker at the private sector hospital to which he had eventually been transferred from prison, they found the therapeutic facilities in that hospital unsatisfactory, particularly in relation to an understanding of ethnic issues (p. 40, cf. discussion of Orville Blackwood's case above). *Third* they recommended 'that social services and district health authorities [should] jointly assess training needs and develop joint training strategies to *promote multi-disciplinary working arrangements* . . . in conjunction with service users and housing and voluntary organisations' (p. 174; emphasis added).

Inquiry into the care and treatment of Christopher Edwards and Richard Linford

This inquiry has an important factor in common with that of the Woodley et al. (1995) report: namely that one 'patient' killed another, but this time in a prison setting. This report (Coonan et al., 1998) is probably one of the most lengthy and comprehensive homicide inquiry reports produced to date. This is because the inquiry panel had, in practice, to conduct two inquiries, into the mental health backgrounds of both men. Richard Linford pleaded guilty to the manslaughter of Christopher Edwards on the grounds of diminished responsibility and was ordered to be detained under Sections 37 and 41 of the Mental Health Act 1983. For various and cogent reasons, the panel took nearly three years to produce their mammoth report. Both men had substantial and lengthy histories of mental disturbance. The inquiry team found that neither of these two highly disturbed men should have been remanded to prison, and certainly not in the same cell, and that there were very serious deficiencies in communication at various stages between the court and the prison to which both of them had been remanded. In addition, the measures taken to oversee their joint safety were deemed to be woefully inadequate and in contravention of the recommendations made by HM Chief Inspector of Prisons: '[Such] cells, which contain integral sanitation, are unsuitable for double occupancy by remand prisoners' (Coonan et al., 1998: 308). Christopher Edwards's parents gave evidence to the inquiry and made a number of complaints about the NHS care of their son. The inquiry found some of these complaints not well founded, but did draw attention to the burden carried by those who are close carers of highly disturbed people. The panel state (p. 25: see also Edwards, P. & Edwards, A., 1998):

> We recognise that a significant burden falls on the relatives of those who suffer mental illness, particularly when there is a reluctance to accept treatment. Mr and Mrs Edwards worked very hard to provide their son with assistance, care and support. They successfully ensured his stability by persuading him to take medication, despite his refusal to accept he was mentally ill.

In both the Robinson and Edwards/Linford cases, close relatives have expressed the view that their opinions or statements were not heeded; in the Robinson case the parents were the 'secondary' victims of the perpetrator and in the Edwards case they were the 'secondary' victims of the homicide victim.[6] Lack of attention to these views and the vital information that close family members can contribute to assessment is the subject of further comment in the following cases.

Inquiry into the treatment and care of Ms B

Ms B pleaded guilty to the manslaughter of her father on the ground of diminished responsibility, and was made subject to a Hospital Order with Restrictions (Sections 37 and 41, Mental Health Act 1983). At the time of the homicide, she was detained under Section 3 of the Act and was on Section 17 leave of absence. Due to problems involved in gaining the patient's consent to access to her medical records and other administrative delays, several weeks elapsed before the independent inquiry got under way. During the course of Ms B's illness there was a conflict of attitude between her parents as to her best interests and how they might be achieved. During the course of the inquiry various criticisms were made by family and friends, notably of the clinical decisions to allow Ms B to be absent without leave on a number of occasions. The inquiry team considered that this criticism was valid and that inadequate precautions were taken to prevent her absconding. In view of the fact that Ms B 'did not wish the hospital staff to make contact with her parents' (Dimond et al., 1997: 22) the inquiry team considered that the hospital acted appropriately since 'The patient is entitled to have information about her condition kept confidential, unless she consents to its disclosure or unless there are legally recognised grounds which do not require the duty to be kept' (p. 23). Such exemption would presumably apply if there was reason to believe that the public interest required it. In view of what the inquiry team have to say about Ms B 'clearly [presenting] a significant risk of serious harm to both herself and others (people known to her and caring for her) . . .' (p. 25) one is left to speculate whether or not this was a case in which the public interest should have overridden the patient's right to confidentiality; the more so, since her father was the eventual victim.

Inquiry into the care and treatment of Martin Mursell

One of the most serious indictments of professionals' lack of concern for the carers of seriously mentally disturbed patients is to be found in the report of the inquiry into the care and management of Martin Mursell. In October 1994, Martin Mursell (age 27), who suffered from schizophrenia, attempted to kill his mother by stabbing, leaving her for dead. He then attacked and killed his stepfather. At his trial for murder and attempted murder, to which he pleaded guilty, he was sentenced to life imprisonment and ten years, the sentences to run concurrently. He was subsequently transferred under the terms of the Mental Health Act to a Special Hospital. In Chapter 7 of their report, the inquiry team stress that 'the needs of carers have been firmly placed at the bottom of priorities of policy makers, health and local authorities, even though the carer's role *is often central* to the life of people with enduring mental illness' (Crawford et al., 1997, p. 86; emphasis added). The report goes on to state (p. 86):

> There was nothing Mrs Collins could have done to avoid being the mother of a schizophrenic son, yet instead of creating a climate in which she felt confident to deal with the problems that she faced, few of the professionals involved with Martin treated her as an equal or showed a sympathetic interest in her plight. She had to deal with conduct and behaviour by Martin which she did not understand and her experience over long periods was very corrosive in the sense of the distress and fear which his behaviour created.

It continues, 'The involvement of the carer in aftercare planning, we suggest must be formalised and incorporated as part of the process of caring for those people with enduring mental illness' (p. 87).

Inquiry into the care of Anthony John Smith (AS)

In August, 1995, Anthony John Smith (AS) killed his mother and his young half-brother. In March the following year, he pleaded guilty to manslaughter and was made subject to a Hospital Order with Restrictions under Sections 37 and 41 of the 1983 Mental Health Act. Concerning consultation and involvement with relatives, the inquiry team had this to say:

> More generally, the lack of communication with AS's family is unfortunate, if possibly explicable. AS appeared to be an adult and self-contained young man; his relatives had not apparently pressed on his admission for an early meeting with the doctors . . . One of the factors that may well have influenced the approach was the

current importance given to confidentiality, for it has to be acknowledged that as AS was an adult there may well have been hesitation
in involving others without explicit permission.

(Wood et al., 1996: 19)

It is interesting to compare this statement with that expressed in the
case of Ms B above (Dimond et al., 1997). However, the Wood inquiry
team (p. 19) went on to make another important point which emphasises
the family's role when looking at the broad context of the patient's
social environment:

> Yet it is the failure to recognise fully the social aspects of AS's
> problems, rather than the medical treatment of his classical psychi-
> atric illness [paranoid schizophrenia], that proved to be one of the
> most important and unfortunate aspects of his care.

Inquiry into the care of Gilbert Kopernik-Steckel

This inquiry is somewhat unusual in that the perpetrator of the
homicide killed himself soon after stabbing his mother to death. At
the Coroner's inquest into the events it was formally recorded that the
perpetrator had a 'psychotic episode at his home address on Sunday,
14 January, 1996. He killed his mother by stabbing her with a knife. He
then took his own life by means of stabbing himself also' (Greenwell
et al., 1997: 1). Gilbert's life up to the time of the fatal incidents had
not been particularly significant psychiatrically, and unlike most of the
other cases described in this chapter, he had not been in and out of the
mental health or criminal justice systems. The report paints a picture of
a somewhat shy, sensitive man, but successful in his chosen profession
of architecture. In 1980 he was referred for psychiatric evaluation
following a conviction for shop-lifting. The specialist who saw him
then considered that he had a severe personality disorder and that Gilbert
was reluctant to continue with the therapeutic treatment that had been
arranged. During a period when he was working in Paris it had been
suggested that he had some kind of breakdown. In the 48 hours from
January 12 to January 14 1996 Gilbert was seen by his GP and the duty
mental health consultant; arrangements were set in hand for him to be
admitted compulsorily for assessment under Section 2 of the 1983 Mental
Health Act. In the event, such admission was not applied for by the
approved social worker, and he was admitted informally on two occasions, but left the hospital on both of them. His family had detected

some slight oddness in his behaviour over the Christmas and New Year period and, following a visit to his GP (who had seen him only once before), it was suggested that he might need some treatment for his depressed feelings. On the morning of January 12 neighbours reported that he had been behaving somewhat oddly and causing a disturbance; the police were called and recognising that he was disturbed, arrested him for breach of the peace with a view to taking him to a place of safety under the Mental Health Act. However, following intervention by his mother, they 'de-arrested' him on condition that she contact the GP. Subsequently, the GP and local psychiatrist visited the home, but the duty approved social worker does not appear to have been informed or asked to attend. They found Gilbert to be 'extremely disturbed' and 'entertaining persecutory delusions'; he had also been drinking heavily. The inquiry team concluded that it ought to have been possible for the two doctors to have talked to Gilbert's mother on her own and she could then have been advised of her rights, as his next of kin, to apply for his compulsory admission. The consultant concerned did not discuss the case with the approved social worker; the inquiry team regarded this as a 'major failure'. During the ensuing weekend, Gilbert's mother indicated that she could cope with him. When Gilbert was in hospital there appears to have been a considerable degree of confusion as to how his case should be handled and, as already stated, he left the hospital on two occasions. Reading the account of events that weekend, one gets the impression of great confusion caused by inadequate communication between nursing and medical staff. Following the tragedy, there appears to have been little attempt to offer help to the remaining family. The inquiry team had this to say:

> We are dismayed to discover that there was no contact with the family from health, social services or the family GP, following the incident. There was not even a letter of condolence, much less an offer of help or support . . . the family had every reason to feel that the statutory agencies had indeed failed and abandoned them.
>
> (Greenwell et al., 1997: 29; see also Rock, 1996, 1998; and Walters, 1998)

Inquiry into the care of Raymond Sinclair

Raymond Sinclair was convicted of the manslaughter (on the grounds of diminished responsibility) of his mother. He was made subject to a Hospital Order with Restrictions under Sections 37 and 41 of the Mental

Health Act 1983. Following the death of his father and his mother's subsequent illness, Raymond Sinclair and the other children in the family were taken into care and eventually placed on supervision orders. As a young adult he had a number of brushes with the law, but no history of assaultive offences. The inquiry report indicates that his behaviour began to deteriorate from 1993 onwards. He had some awareness of his deteriorating mental health, sought support from his brother and mother (on whom he became increasingly dependent), from the church, 'in which he became obsessively involved . . . and eventually went to his family doctor as his hallucinations became increasingly frightening, abusive and threatening' (Lingham et al., 1996: 14). In 1994 he had various admissions to psychiatric hospital. The inquiry team comment on the fact that too much weight was given to Raymond Sinclair's own reassurances that he would stay in hospital. He was allowed to return home to his mother who lived *in a one-roomed flat*; one of Sinclair's brothers was also living there on a temporary basis. The inquiry expressed the family's concern in powerful terms:

> The principal message left with us by the family members is their continuing anger and astonishment that it was possible for someone as manifestly ill, disturbed and dependent as Raymond Sinclair to be discharged from hospital on the first occasion to the care of their semi-mobile, sixty-four-year old mother living in a small flat which was designed for an elderly single person or couple at most . . . They thought that the statutory services depended heavily on family members but had not actively involved them in planning or providing for his needs . . . for members of the . . . family it is particularly appropriate to demonstrate how badly they felt let down by the health and social services for a failure, as they see it, to provide sufficient protective care.
>
> (Lingham et al., 1996: 62–3)

Inquiry into the death of Brenda Horrod

In May 1995, Peter Horrod pleaded guilty to the manslaughter (on the grounds of diminished responsibility) of his disabled wife Brenda, and was made the subject of a Hospital Order with Restrictions under Sections 37 and 41 of the Mental Health Act 1983. During 1994 and 1995 he had been an in-patient at a psychiatric hospital in Great Yarmouth, Norfolk. It would appear that he had been prematurely discharged from that hospital by a junior doctor; following that discharge, he killed his wife. At his trial, his counsel made the following statement in mitigation on his client's behalf:

> It seems to me to be futile and unattractive if one starts casting blame. The fact is that this man, twenty-four hours before he killed his wife, was discharged back home at 2.30 in the morning [by taxi], having just taken an overdose, with two lengthy periods of hospitalisation behind him. What on earth people thought they were doing sending him back home is one of the tragedies of this case.
>
> (Armstrong et al., 1998: 26)

In view of the fact that Peter Horrod's wife was severely disabled, one might have thought that there would have been close professional support for the family. The inquiry team seem to suggest otherwise (p. 24):

> Communications with relatives and carers of patients does not appear to have been given priority and was certainly not the subject of any established procedure. Whilst it was clearly accepted that consulting with relatives was a desirable practice, the fact that it happened at all seems to have been the result of initiatives taken by relatives and carers rather than medical or nursing staff being pro-active in seeking out the views of relatives. This was a major shortcoming. No-one knows a patient better than their relatives and carers and procedures should be in place to ensure that their views are not only listened to when received but also actively sought out.

DO ANY THEMES EMERGE?

Some of my readers may consider that my choice of inquiries in this chapter is somewhat idiosyncratic. I acknowledge this, but in my defence I would assert that my aim has been to provide a *range* of investigations from what is now, sadly, a vast number of inquiries held in the past two decades. Because of their somewhat diverse nature, it would be stupidly dogmatic to present over-precise themes. However, it seems to me that certain themes *do* emerge, and I now identify a few of these before proceeding to deal with the purposes, procedures and the future of inquiries more generally. The themes, only adumbrated here, will also serve as a springboard for further discussion in the final chapter.

1   One's overall impression from the foregoing reports is that we still have a long way to go in encouraging mental health and criminal justice professionals to take a broad view of an individual's social functioning in relation to their illness. This may arise, *in part*, because of the tendency for medical practitioners to play a dominant role in the practice of psychiatry. To some extent this is understandable, given that in cases governed by the mental health legislation the Responsible Medical Officer (RMO) is held responsible in law for acts of negligence or omission (see also Reith, 1998a, Chapter 4).

2   The importance of matching past behaviour to present behaviour has often been overlooked. More needs to be done in encouraging workers to compile careful chronologies of patients' lives.

3   Linked with point 2 is the need for the maintenance of adequate records and the development of common systems of recording. For the most part, each mental health and criminal justice service has its own system of record keeping.

4   Too little attention is being paid to acknowledging the importance of vulnerability in the assessment and management of risk; the importance, that is, of not placing patients and offenders back into situations which may promote the commission of further disastrous actions, and the completion of what the late Dr Murray Cox called 'unfinished business'.

5   There is a compelling need to develop more sensitivity to issues of race, culture and gender differences. Most racism in institutions, be they opened or closed, operates at a subliminal level (see Macpherson, 1999).

6   Workers need to develop what I would call a more 'robust' approach to dealing with offenders and offender–patients. Concern for civil liberties has sometimes obscured the need to place public protection at the forefront. A more searching, questioning stance is needed, a matter to be addressed in the final chapter.

7   Levels and modes of communication between professionals still leave a lot to be desired. Top–down approaches to care and management are still too prevalent; sharing of information is still not as good as it might be and workers are often defensive, believing that 'Knowledge is power'. There is too much of a tendency to hide behind confidentiality as a defence to information sharing, as is the tendency to 'go it alone'.

8   Finally, the roles played by, and support for, family and other close carers have not been adequately addressed – sometimes with tragic consequences.

HOMICIDE INQUIRIES: CURRENT GUIDANCE

As already noted, current guidance is laid down by the Department of Health NHS Executive (*Guidance on the discharge of mentally disordered people and their care in the community, HSG/94/27*, 1994). The essential elements of the Departmental instructions are as follows:

In cases of homicide, it will always be necessary for the District Health Authority to hold an independent inquiry. The only exception is where the victim is a child; here separate regulations apply. In establishing an independent inquiry, the following points should be taken into account:

THE REMIT OF THE INQUIRY

This should encompass at least:

- The care and treatment the patient was receiving at the time of the incident.
- The suitability of the care in view of the patient's history and assessed health and social care needs.
- The extent to which that care corresponded with statutory obligations.
- The exercise of professional judgement.
- The adequacy of the care plan and its monitoring by the responsible worker.

COMPOSITION OF THE INQUIRY PANEL

Consideration should be given to appointing as chairman an independent person (who need not be a lawyer). Other members should include a psychiatrist, and if appropriate, a senior representative from social services and/or a senior nurse and/or a senior health service manager.

THE DISTRIBUTION OF THE ENQUIRY REPORT

An undertaking, given at the start of the process, to publish the report will enhance the credibility of the inquiry. In exceptional cases, it may not be desirable for the final report to be made public. In these circumstances, an undertaking should be given at the start of the inquiry that the main findings will be made available to interested parties.

CURRENT PRACTICE

Most inquiries have followed the general guidelines outlined above, and most set out in some detail the procedures the panel propose to adopt. They give, for example, a detailed statement of the inquiry's remit, the manner in which witnesses will be asked to give oral and/or written evidence, and arrangements for representation and opportunities for witnesses to respond to any criticisms that might be levelled at them. Because the central government guidance does not set boundaries as to the extent of an inquiry's remit this has led inquiry panels to settle this matter for themselves. A number of panels have commented on the need for firmer guidance, since its absence can lead to difficulties. For example, in the inquiry I chaired into the care and management of Sanjay Kumar Patel (Prins et al., 1998), both the social services and the education department were unhappy that we had extended our remit to cover their services to Sanjay Patel in his childhood and adolescence (Sanjay was 19 when he committed the homicide – the killing of a vagrant in the centre of Leicester). We set out our reasoning in this matter in the following terms:

> It was borne in upon the panel during the course of this inquiry how difficult it was to draw fine dividing lines between the functions of the various agencies involved. In this case, there are a number of areas where inter-agency overlap is unavoidable. This may be particularly relevant for this type of inquiry when it involves the mental health of children and adolescents whose needs are also addressed by other legislation and when young people are in transition between services for children and adolescents and those for adults . . . The panel has sought to identify the quality of care given to Sanjay Patel by the various agencies and the level of collaboration and co-operation that there was between them. When undertaking this inquiry, the panel had in mind the importance of seeking out, not only the key events in this tragic event so that lessons can be learned from them, but *to highlight these for the information of all those who will have responsibilities for [his] care and management in the future* [emphasis added].
> (Prins et al., 1998: 3; see also Dimond et al., 1997: 36, para 3)

So far as I am aware, few, if any, other inquiry reports have stressed the matters I have placed in emphasis; some may consider that this goes beyond the panel's remit. My colleagues and I chose, we think for good reason, to think otherwise.

Inquiries are expensive, be they held in private or in public. If in public, the costs will mount considerably since representation of all parties to the inquiry will be necessary. Most homicide inquiries have been held in private – wisely in my view. In public inquiries, the proceedings tend inevitably to operate on an adversarial as opposed to an inquisitorial basis. Decisions to hold them in private or in public seem somewhat arbitrary. For example, the inquiry into the care and treatment of Christopher Clunis (which has served as something of a model for all subsequent inquiries) chose to sit in private, as did the inquiry into the death of the young carer, Jonathan Newby (Davies et al., 1995). The inquiries into the Robinson and Mitchell cases were held in public. I can find no evidence that either of these latter inquiries would have been hampered in any way had they been held in private. There are good reasons for believing that private hearings allow witnesses to give sensitive and often emotive evidence and to feel less constrained and stressed. At a fairly recent conference on the future of inquiries, the Responsible Medical Officer in the Mitchell case gave a most moving account of the impact of the inquiry on himself and his family; for him it was clearly a traumatic experience, for even if no blame attaches, the professional is likely to feel, perhaps quite irrationally, that they may be to blame. In some way this is more likely to be the case if the hearings are in the full glare of public scrutiny.

Some feel that fairness also demands that the perpetrator of the homicide (who at the time of the inquiry will have been convicted and sentenced) should be asked to consent to all the personal documentation in their case being made available to the inquiry team; in a number of instances this has been done and consent obtained. An opposing view is that in such 'public interest' cases, consent is not required, the view being that difficulties would arise if consent was withheld. The Mitchell (Blom-Cooper et al., 1996) and Dimond et al. (1997) inquiry teams suggested that central government should give clearer direction in this matter; namely that disclosure in the public interest should be seen to include disclosure to an inquiry.

PUBLICATION AND DISTRIBUTION OF REPORTS

Both these matters require some degree of rationalisation. For example, some reports are published in good quality glossy format by the commissioning authority (such as a health authority, either alone, or in conjunction with a social service, probation, police or prison authority); and some are published as Command papers by authority of Parliament and printed by the Stationery Office. One or two inquiry reports have been published commercially as books (two notable examples being the reports into the Robinson and Mitchell cases). Such general publication will ensure a wide and more accessible readership.

However, ensuring such a wide readership may encourage an inquiry team to stray beyond their original remit and make much wider recommendations than the task required. Such tendencies are not new; Grounds (1997) makes the point that similar wide-ranging recommendations were being made into cases of alleged psychiatric-hospital–patient abuse in the late 1960s. Occasionally, reports are published in-house in cyclostyled paper covers; these seem to do less than justice to the matters being investigated and to the work involved in doing so. Failure, for whatever reason, to print enough copies or to reprint them – as was the case in our inquiry into Orville Blackwood's death in Broadmoor (Prins et al., 1993) – means that, at both time of publication and subsequently, legitimate enquirers are denied access.

There is also the question of dissemination of inquiry reports. They appear in serial fashion and many of them make very similar recommendations. Following such action as the authorities choose to take at local level, the report is then most likely shelved. As Reith says 'The information that is already available needs to be made more accessible by a central body such as the Department of Health so that the available information [e.g. in cumulative inquiry reports] is properly disseminated' (Reith, 1998c: 17). Crichton and Sheppard (1996: 71) express the problem in sharper terms:

> If the current rash of inquiry reports are not widely read and do not influence practice, then they risk being as nationally relevant as a private stamp collection . . . if they are dismissed before they are read and fail to engender a debate of the issues, then a valuable opportunity for improving national practice will be lost.

Finally, some inquiry teams sign the report (usually at the front); others do not. There seems little justification for signatures appearing on the printed copies; if signatures are deemed necessary, they can be appended to the master copy.

PURPOSE OF INQUIRIES

Sir Louis Blom-Cooper, who has chaired many inquiries into abuses of one kind or another, including homicides, concludes that the purpose of inquiries is 'to examine the truth . . . what happened . . . how did it happen, and who if anyone was responsible, culpably or otherwise, for it having happened?' (Blom-Cooper, 1993: 20). So far so good, but are there not problems in such a definition of purpose and are there not, indeed, other purposes, explicit or implicit? The search for truth is admirable, but is it as readily ascertainable as might be inferred from Sir Louis' remarks? All of us who work in this field agree that it is very easy to be wise after the event, and that 'hindsight bias' may lead one to draw facile or quite erroneous conclusions – hence the insertion of the word 'Doubtful' in the title of this chapter. Coonan et al. (1998: 3) put the problem in very balanced context. They state:

> The essential requirement is that the Inquiry should be fair and just; to be seen to be fair and just; and at the same time provide answers to the fundamental questions: 'How?' and 'Why?' the death occurred. A balance must be struck between the competing demands of the inquisitorial nature of the Inquiry and the requirement to provide some degree of protection to individuals whose credibility and competence is strongly impugned. Serious allegations had been made against specific individuals at the outset. Provided the correct balance is struck, the requirements of seeking the truth, making recommendations, and at the same time identifying individual failure, where appropriate, is both reconcilable and achievable.[7]

As far as I am aware, no homicide inquiry report has stated categorically that omissions or failures in practice could be shown *conclusively* to have caused the homicidal event. The best that can be said is that such failures *may* have been contributory factors. This has led some to question the desirability of such complex, costly and time-consuming procedures. However, it has to be stressed that inquiries into homicides are needed, not just to inquire into practices and offer necessary criticism. They are also needed for the purposes of public catharsis, most notably to help the families of the deceased (and in some cases of the perpetrator) to cope with their grief. (See Reder & Duncan, 1996, and Rock, 1996; 1998). Grounds (1997: 134) suggests that 'Families have two overriding concerns; first, that they should know what happened, even if the process of learning is an ordeal; secondly, [that] what happened to them should not happen to others in the future'.

TIME FOR CHANGE

A number of authorities have expressed the view that changes are required in the present system of inquiries. Eastman advocates 'That the main purpose of inquiries should be pursued separately. This implies that inquiries should investigate only causal explanation and should always be explicitly precluded from expressing a judgement about *professional culpability*' (Eastman, 1996: 1070; emphasis added). He suggests that judgements about the latter should always be made either through the professional's governing body or through the civil courts.

A further deficiency in the present system must be mentioned. Currently, each inquiry is a single event; the team carry out their mandated tasks and present their report. It is then left to the authorities being reviewed to accept or reject whatever recommendations are made, and to act upon them as they see fit. Very rarely is a panel asked to revisit to ensure that their recommendations have been implemented. Indeed, there seems to be some reluctance to accept such offers, as we found in our inquiry into Orville Blackwood's death in Broadmoor (Prins et al., 1993).

The possibilities of loss of useful information through the absence of an effective channel of dissemination was referred to earlier. What direction then should future policy and practice take? I would suggest the following:

- Mandatory homicide inquiries should either cease or, if they are not abandoned entirely, there should be some clear time limit set on how long ago the perpetrator was in contact with the mental health services. At present, this appears to be limitless and is left to the discretion of individual panels to determine. This is highly unsatisfactory.
- In the event of formal inquiries being abandoned, there should be set in place more effective systems of monitoring and audit, notably in respect of risk assessment and management (see Eastman, 1996).[8] There should be a requirement to report all homicide cases, perhaps to the Department of Health. That (or some other body) would then decide if an independent external inquiry was required.
- Such residual cases should then become the responsibility of a central body (such as the Mental Health Act Commission) who could maintain a register of possible inquiry team members and also act as an inquiry secretariat (see Bingley, 1996). An official

body (HAS, 2000) has been asked by the Department of Health to develop standards and guidelines for the pattern of future inquiries (Zito Trust, 1999).

CONCLUDING COMMENTS

Petch and Bradley (1997: 182)[9] have some apposite observations that can usefully serve as a conclusion to this chapter:

> It has not yet been established why psychiatric patients kill others ... However, many inquiries and their reports imply there is something the psychiatric services can do to prevent this happening. The implication is that if a gold standard of care was provided, psychiatric patients would either not kill other people or would do so less frequently. This is far from certain, but if there are things which services can do to reduce the likelihood of homicides by psychiatric patients, the lessons must be learned.

The manner in which services can try to assist in preventing such events is the subject of my final chapter.

NOTES

1 There are a number of other cases that are germane to the discussion in this chapter. They are not included here because they did not, as far as I can ascertain, result in an inquiry. One example is that of Christopher Simcox, who killed on two occasions, in the early 1950s and in the 1960s, following release from his first life sentence. He subsequently killed his sister-in-law and wounded another of his wife's relatives. The other example is that of Terrence John Illiffe who, in 1974, was sentenced to life imprisonment for the murder by strangulation of his fourth wife. He subsequently hid her body in their deep-freezer. The killing was carried out within a year of his release from Broadmoor, where he had been committed in 1970 for causing grievous bodily harm to his then wife. The assessments made at the time of his discharge from hospital gave no reason to believe that he would present any general risk to the public. However, it was appreciated that 'if Illiffe were to remarry, there might be a specific risk to his wife' (Home Office & Department of Health and Social Security, 1975). Those responsible for his supervision recognised that if he indicated any such intention his 'prospective wife must be fully informed of his background'. What was not foreseen, however, was

that he might marry *without the knowledge of his supervising officer*. When this marriage was discovered, attempts were made to inform the wife, 'but tragically to no avail'. See Prins, 1995: 233 for fuller accounts of these two cases.

2 Bowden's article provides a fascinating insight into Young's history and psychopathology. See also Holden's account for further background details and discussion (Holden, 1995); and the account by Young's Aunt Winifred (Young, 1973).

3 The observations in this section are based on a report prepared by the Bridge Consultancy. The report is a broad *overview*. Detailed case information was not made public due to two High Court injunctions aimed at protecting the children in the West family and because of medical confidentiality. As is now well known, Rosemary West was convicted on ten counts of murder and sentenced to life imprisonment. Her husband, Fred, committed suicide whilst awaiting trial. For biographical accounts of both of them, see Masters (1996); Wansell (1996); and Burn (1998).

4 The descriptions of the cases of Barratt and Kim Kirkman draw quite heavily on those provided by Reith (1998). See also a recent interesting paper reviewing eleven independent homicide inquiries by Lipsedge and Bland (1997).

5 The tragic consequences of inadequate or complete lack of training are exemplified in the report into the circumstances leading to the death of Jonathan Newby – a volunteer worker in an Oxford mental aftercare hostel dealing with highly disturbed residents (Davies et al., 1995).

6 Rock has described the needs and wishes of 'secondary victims' (relatives) in very sensitive fashion: 'At the forefront is the gap that can yawn between the rational reasoned, universalistic, precedent-driven and cool talk of the professional and the impassioned, particularistic and hot talk of some survivors' representatives, two kinds of talk that cannot sustain a coherent conversation for very long' (Rock, 1998: 198; see also Rock, 1996).

7 An excellent critical perspective on inquiries, their purposes and impact, may be found in Chapter 19 of *Managing high security psychiatric care* (Kaye & Franey, 1998).

8 For an interesting account of how clinical audit may be made more effective, see Marks (1998).

9 Although Petch and Bradley's remarks are directed at homicides committed by psychiatric patients, what they say is capable of extrapolation to homicides committed by persons known to other services. For an example of such a case involving the Probation Service, see Scotland et al. (1998).

REFERENCES

Aarvold, Sir Carl, Hill, Sir Denis, & Newton, G.P. (1973). *Report on the review of procedures into the discharge of psychiatric patients subject to special restrictions* (Cmnd 5191). London: HMSO.

Appleby, L., Shaw, J. & Amos, T. (1997). National confidential inquiry into suicide and homicide by people with mental illness. *British Journal of Psychiatry, 170,* 101–2.

Armstrong, W., Calloway, P., Arnold, M., & Schofield, T. (1998). *Report of the independent inquiry into the circumstances leading to the death of Brenda Horrod.* Norwich: East Norfolk Health Authority.

Bingley, W. (1996). Hospital inquiries: Have we learned anything? *Criminal Behaviour and Mental Health* (Suppl.): 5–10.

Blom-Cooper, Sir L. QC. (1993). Public Inquiries. In M. Freeman & B. Hepple (eds), *Current legal problems.* Oxford: Oxford University Press.

Blom-Cooper, Sir L. QC, Hally, H., & Murphy, E. (1995). *The falling shadow: One patient's mental health care (1978–1993).* London: Duckworth.

Blom-Cooper, Sir L. QC, Grounds, A., Guinan, P., Parker, A., & Taylor, M. (1996). *The case of Jason Mitchell: Report of the independent panel of inquiry.* London: Duckworth.

Bowden, P. (1996). Graham Young (1947–1990), the St. Albans poisoner: His life and times. *Criminal Behaviour and Mental Health* (Suppl.): 17–24.

Bridge Child Care Consultancy Service. (1995). *Report prepared for Gloucestershire Area Child Protection Committee, Part 8 case review: overview report in respect of Charmaine and Heather West.* Gloucester: Gloucester County Council Social Services Department.

Burn G. (1998). *Happy like murderers.* London: Faber and Faber.

Chapman, H., Ashman, M., Oyebode, O., & Rogers, B. (1996). *Report of the independent inquiry into the treatment and care of Richard John Burton.* Leicester: Leicestershire Health Authority.

Clothier, Sir Cecil, QC, Macdonald, C.A., & Shaw, D.A. (1994). *The Allitt inquiry: Independent inquiry relating to the deaths and injuries on the childrens' ward at Grantham and Kesteven General Hospital during the period February–April, 1991.* London: HMSO.

Coonan, K. QC, Bluglass, R., Halliday, G., Jenkins, M., & Kelly, O. (1998). *Report of the inquiry into the care and treatment of Christopher Edwards and Richard Linford.* Chelmsford, Essex: North Essex Health Authority, Essex County Council, HM Prison Service and Essex Police.

Crawford, L., Devaux, M., Ferris, R., & Hayward, P. (1997). *The Report into the care and treatment of Martin Mursell.* London: Camden and Islington Health Authority.

Crichton, J., & Sheppard, D. (1996). Psychiatric inquiries: Learning the lessons. In J. Peay (ed.), *Inquiries after homicide.* London: Duckworth.

Davies, N., Lingham, R., Prior, C., & Sims, A. (1995). *Report of the inquiry into the circumstances leading to the death of Jonathan Newby (a volunteer worker) on 9 October, 1993.* Oxford: Oxford Health Authority.

Department of Health NHS Executive (*Guidance on the discharge of mentally disordered people and their case in the community, HSG/94/27,* 1994), London.

Dick, D., Shuttleworth, B., & Charlton, J. (1991). *Report of the panel of inquiry appointed by the West Midlands Regional Health Authority, South Birmingham Health Authority and the Special Hospitals Service Authority to investigate the case of Kim Kirkman*. Birmingham: West Midlands Health Authority.

Dimond, B., Bowden, P., Sallah, D., Holden, R., & Lingham, R. (1997). *Summary of the report of the inquiry into the care and treatment of Ms B*. Avon: Avon Health Authority.

Eastman, N. (1996). Inquiry into homicides by psychiatric patients: Systematic audit should replace mandatory inquiries. *British Medical Journal 313*, 1069–71.

Edwards, P., & Edwards, A. (1998). Recognising responsibilities to families. In A. Liebling (ed.), *Deaths of offenders: The hidden side of justice*, Winchester: Waterside Press (in Conjunction with Institute for the Study and Treatment of Delinquency, London).

Greenwell, J., Procter, A., & Jones, A. (1997). *Report of the inquiry into the treatment and care of Gilbert Kopernik-Steckel*. Croydon: Croydon Health Authority.

Grounds, A. (1997). Commentary on inquiries: Who needs them? *Psychiatric Bulletin, 21*, 134–5.

Heginbotham, C., Carr, J., Hale, R., Walsh, T., & Warrant, C. (1994). *Report of the independent panel of inquiry examining the care of Michael Buchanan*. Brent Park, London: North West London Mental Health NHS Trust.

Holden, A. (1995) *The St Albans poisoner: The life and crimes of Graham Young* (2nd ed.). London: Corgi Books.

Home Office & Department of Health and Social Security. (1975). *Report of the committee of inquiry on mentally abnormal offenders* (Cmnd 6244, Butler Committee). London: HMSO.

Kaye, C., & Franey, A. (eds). (1998). *Managing high security psychiatric care*. London: Jessica Kingsley.

Lingham, R., Candy J., & Bray, J. (1996). *Report of the inquiry into the treatment and care of Raymond Sinclair*. Maidstone: West Kent Health Authority and Kent County Council Social Services Department.

Lipsedge, M. & Bland, S.R. (1997). Review of 11 independent inquiries into homicide by psychiatric patients. *Clinical Risk, 3*, 171–7.

Macpherson, Sir W. (1999). *The Stephen Lawrence inquiry* (Advisers, Cook, T., Sentamu, J., & Stone, R.). Cmnd 426(1) and (2) (Vols 1–2). London: HMSO.

Marks, I. (1998). Overcoming obstacles to routine outcome measurements: The nuts and bolts of implementing clinical audit. *British Journal of Psychiatry, 173*, 281–6.

Masters, B. (1996). *She must have known: The trial of Rosemary West*. London: Doubleday.

Petch, E. & Bradley, C. (1997). Learning the lessons from homicide inquiries: Adding insult to injury. *Journal of Forensic Psychiatry, I*, 161–84.

Prins, H., Backer-Holst, T., Francis, E., & Keitch, I. (1993). *Report of the committee of inquiry into the death in Broadmoor Hospital of Orville*

Blackwood and a review of the deaths of two other Afro-Caribbean patients: 'Big, black and dangerous?' London: Special Hospitals Service Authority.

Prins, H., Marshall, A., & Day, K. (1997). *Report of the independent panel of inquiry into the circumstances surrounding the absconsion of Mr Holland from the care of the Horizon NHS Trust on 19 August 1996.* Harperbury, Hertfordshire: Horizon NHS Trust.

Prins, H., Ashman, M., Steele, G., & Swann, M. (1998). *Report of the independent panel of inquiry into the treatment and care of Sanjay Kumar Patel.* Leicester: Leicestershire Health Authority.

Reder, P., & Duncan, S. (1996). Reflections on child abuse inquiries. In J. Peay (ed.), *Inquiries after homicide.* London: Duckworth.

Reith, M. (1998a). *Community care tragedies: A practical guide to mental health inquiries.* Birmingham: Venture Press.

Reith, M. (1998b). Risk assessment and management: Lessons from mental health inquiry reports. *Medicine, Science and the Law, 38,* 221–6.

Reith, M. (1998c). Why we have had enough inquiries into care tragedies. *Professional Social Work,* August, 16–17.

Ritchie, J., Dick, D., & Lingham, R. (1994). *The report of the inquiry into the care and treatment of Christopher Clunis.* London: HMSO.

Rock, P. (1996). The inquiry and victims' families'. In J. Peay (ed.), *Inquiries after homicide.* London: Duckworth.

Rock, P. (1998). Murderers, victims and 'survivors'. *British Journal of Criminology, 38,* 185–200.

Scotland, P.C. (Baroness), Kelly K., & Devaux, M. (1998). *The report of the Luke Warm Luke mental health inquiry* (Vols 1–2). London: Lambeth, Southwark and Lewisham Health Authority.

Scottish Office. (1996). *The public inquiry into the shootings at Dublane Primary School on 13 March 1996* (Cmnd 3300) (Cullen Report). London and Edinburgh: HMSO.

Sheppard, D. (1996). *Learning the lessons* (2nd ed.). London: Zito Trust.

Spokes, J.C., Pare, M., & Royle, G. (1998). *Report of the committee of inquiry into the aftercare of Miss Sharon Campbell* (Cmnd 440). London: HMSO.

Steering Committee of the confidential inquiry into homicides and suicides by mentally ill people. (1994). *Preliminary Report.* London: Royal College of Psychiatrists.

Steering Committee of the confidential inquiry into homicides and suicides by mentally ill people. (1996). *Final Report.* London: Royal College of Psychiatrists.

Unwin, C., Morgan, D.H., & Smith, B.D.M. (1991). *Regional fact finding committee of inquiry into the administration, care, treatment and discharge of Carol Barratt.* Sheffield: Trent Regional Health Authority.

Wansell, G. (1996). *An evil love: The life of Frederick West.* London: Headline.

Wiltshire County Council. (1988). *Report of a departmental inquiry into the discharge of responsibilities of Wiltshire Social Services in relation to Daniel*

Mudd from his release from Broadmoor in May 1983 until his arrest in December 1986 for the murder of Ruth Perrett. Trowbridge: Author.

Walters, J. (1998). Victim perspectives and implications for work with offenders. *Vista, 4,* 2–10.

Wood, Sir John, Ashman, M., Davies, C., Lloyd, H., & Lockett, K. (1996). *Report of the inquiry into the care of Anthony Smith.* Derby: Southern Derbyshire Health Authority and Derbyshire County Council.

Woodley, L. QC, Dixon, K., Lindow, V., Oyebote, C., Stanford T., & Simblet, S. (1995). *Report of the independent review panel following a homicide in July 1994 by a person suffering from a severe mental illness.* London: East London and the City Health Authority and Newham Council.

Young, W. (1973). *Obsessive poisoner: The strange story of Graham Young.* London: Robert Hale.

Zito Trust. (1997a). *Community care homicides since 1990* (1st ed.). London: Author.

Zito Trust. (1997b). *Journal, 2,* October. London: Author.

Zito Trust. (1998a). *Journal, 3,* February. London: Author.

Zito Trust. (1998b). *Journal, 4,* July. London: Author.

Zito Trust. (1999). *ZT Monitor, 6,* March/April. London: Author.

Chapter 5

Improving practice

How dangerous is it that this man goes loose?

(*Hamlet*, IV, iii)

To assume that a bad outcome implies a bad decision is the most fundamental and widespread of all fallacies.

(Dowie, 1990)

Clinical assessment is not primarily about making an accurate prediction but about making informed *defensible* decisions about dangerous behaviour.

(Grounds, 1995)

CONTEXT

At various points in this book I have tried to provide illustrations of instances where, with the benefit of hindsight, we can see that risk assessment and management might have been improved. Merely to point out some of those errors and omissions would be a failure on my part to make suggestions for improvements in practice. This chapter is devoted therefore to some consideration of these issues. Although it focuses mainly on what might best be described as clinical deficiencies, this should in no way be taken to be an indication that failures in the provision of resources are not of crucial concern. One of the key findings to emerge with alarming frequency in many of the reports referred to in the last chapter is the lack of adequate resourcing of mental health services of all kinds and at all levels. However, only very recently have there been hints of a greater degree of political awareness of such needs and some degree of determination to do something about them. Kemshall (1996: 71; see also Kemshall, 1999; Crighton, 1999) puts the issues into perspective when she states:

Most services are currently struggling with the issues of prioritisation and clearer messages on risk in a context within which existing cultures and traditions die hard. This can result in significant gaps between management and expectations and front-line risk decisions.

This view is given added emphasis by Carson (1995: 76):

'Risk Management' needs to be understood in [the] pro-active sense of establishing frameworks and standards for decision making rather than just the relatively more reactive meaning findings ways of reducing the likelihood and seriousness of consequences.[1]

The rest of this chapter is devoted to the following matters: problems of prediction of risk; ethical issues; aspects of communication; working from an effective baseline; and enhancing good practice.

PREDICTION

Gunn (1996) has traced something of the recent preoccupation with the prediction of violence. He compares this with the manner in which the BBC Meteorological Office aimed to make accurate weather predictions, but found that (unsurprisingly) whilst it was possible to make fairly accurate short-term predictions (e.g. 2+ hours), it was almost impossible to make them long term, even when these were based on a careful statistical analysis of previous weather patterns over many years. From this fact a very useful lesson can be derived, namely that in the criminal justice and mental health fields, although it *may* be possible to make *short-term* predictions about the commission of future violence, in the *long term* this is much more hazardous. There is also another important issue to be addressed. For many years, professionals in the criminal justice and mental health fields have taken comfort from the much cited (but usually unascribed) quotation from the American psychologist Kvaraceus that 'nothing predicts behaviour like behaviour' (1966: 6). As Gunn (1996: 53) suggests, this shows a fundamental misunderstanding of statistical analysis; he suggests that such analysis is 'constantly reinforced by [the use of] retrospective statistical data', and continues:

The problem is that whilst statistics, which are mathematical extrapolations from group activity, can be extremely powerful in describing and perhaps predicting group activity [although that needs to be tested prospectively, not retrospectively], they cannot tell us which members of which group will do what.

Workers, such as Webster and his colleagues, have endeavoured to combine actuarial and clinical approaches. In attempting to answer the question *Can violent acts be predicted?* they state:

> From a scientific perspective [the question] is impossible to answer since it is based upon an unscientific assumption about dangerousness, namely that it is a stable and consistent quality existing within the individual.

They suggest that a translation into more appropriate terms would produce the following question:

> What are the psychological, social and biological factors bearing on the defendant's ... behaviour and what are the implications for future (behaviour) and the potential for change?
>
> (Pollock & Webster, 1991: 493)[2]

Many workers have suggested that 'statistical studies of the prediction of dangerousness ... indicate a high rate of error, usually in the direction of over-prediction' (Greenland, 1980: 99). However, Greenland also reminds us that 'much less attention is paid to the havoc caused by the "false positives". These are the patients who kill or maim people after being considered *safe* for discharge'. Criminal justice and mental health professionals (particularly psychiatrists) have been frequently criticised for making apparently unrealistic claims to expertise in the assessment of dangerousness. Greenland suggests that a number of these criticisms are ill-founded. He bases his assertion largely on the grounds that psychiatrists are no worse than other professionals in making such predictions, and that when given the task of predicting risk in *mentally ill* offenders they are able to offer considerable expertise.

Greenland's views are supported by Gunn (1996: 54) in the paper already referred to, who states:

> If psychiatrists are asked to make predictions about behaviour over long periods of time, they are bound to be wrong quite often and they are bound, given their responsibilities, to be cautious about the predictions they make and over-predict rather than under-predict. Yet, like the weather forecasters, whilst they often get the long-range prediction wrong, they are not bad at the short-term ... whether Bill Bloggs is going to be violent again in three or four years' time

or even within the next six months, is much less important than whether he is going to be violent in the next week or two . . .

In the final analysis, there are no statistical or actuarial measures available that offer the prediction of dangerous behaviour in either (so-called) normal or mentally disturbed offenders with any real degree of certainty. Despite the fact that considerable research has been carried out into the prediction of anti-social behaviour generally, this has merely tended to indicate that, although actuarial techniques can discriminate between high-risk and low-risk groups, there will always be a residual majority in the middle-risk groups whose re-offending rates are too near fifty-fifty to be of much use prognostically in individual cases. (For a recent study of antecedent factors in relation to risk assessment, see Strand et al., 1999.) In the absence of firm research indicators, practitioners are left to carry the burdens of decision making in anxiety producing cases. Such burdens are very real. For example, Street (1998), in his impressive study of the community supervision of Restriction Order Patients (Sections 37/41 Mental Health Act 1983), found that in nearly a third of his conditional discharge cases (n=115), a social supervisor expressed concern about the *possible* risk posed by patients 'on occasions separate to any re-offending or harmful incidents'. 'In 86 per cent of these cases the concern was general, based, for example, on circumstances arising that were similar to those surrounding the index offence.' Sometimes the anxiety was made worse by an ambiguous context; for example, where 'the basis for the concern included specific incidents, including a few cases where allegations were made about harmful behaviour by the patients but quickly retracted, or subsequently proved to be false . . .' (Street, 1998: 81). It can be said with some justification that ambiguity and uncertainty are the order of the day in risk assessment and management. The ambiguity and uncertainty are compounded by the need to try to reconcile the needs of the offender/offender–patient on the one hand, and society on the other. The dilemma produced by these conflicting demands produces ethical issues of some importance. Some of these are now considered.

ETHICAL ISSUES

General aspects

As already indicated, risk assessment and management frequently consist of trying to balance the needs of the individual offender/offender–patient against the protection of the public. Professor Nigel Walker

(1982) has given a great deal of thought to this dilemma and has written extensively on the subject. What now follows draws heavily upon his work. First of all, he alerts us to the fact that, given the inadequacies of the predictive devices and skills referred to above, we are likely to detain individuals in prisons or hospitals on the grounds of their potential dangerousness for far longer than we would on tariff grounds alone. In order to try to limit the need for such detention, Walker proposed what he described as a set of five 'non-arithmetical rules', as follows:

1   He suggests the exclusion of most property offenders and those cases which he describes as causing temporary alarm such as minor threats to decency; for example, indecent exposure. However, in my view, this latter exclusion seems slightly questionable, since the offence of indecent exposure can, under certain circumstances, cause considerable psychological trauma. Moreover, a small proportion of indecent exposers go on to commit more serious sexual crimes (see later).

2   Walker suggests that what he describes as isolated out-of-character acts should not be included. Previous similar conduct would help to establish whether or not a pattern existed as, for example, declared intentions of future vengeance. (See, for example, the discussion of aspects of jealousy in Chapter 3.)

3   Rule 3 would operate to an offender's advantage if (a) the incentives for his or her initial offending ceased to exist, or (b) through incapacity, he or she was unlikely to repeat the conduct. However, it would seem prudent to observe that the first criterion might be less easy to implement than the latter, since it is not unknown for those who have killed to find surrogate victims.

4   More use should be made of close monitoring and supervision in the community (see later). In addition, with his usual foresight, Walker suggests barring some offenders from certain employments (for example, work with children; see Walker, 1991).

5   Finally, Walker suggests that for those who need to be incarcerated for long periods, their detention should be as humane and progressive as possible. Current concerns about prison overcrowding and the criticisms of treatment regimes in certain of our Special Hospitals seem to indicate that Walker's laudable suggestion may be difficult to implement.

When and to whom to tell

One of the most problematic areas for practitioners dealing with potentially dangerous offenders and offender–patients is when and in what circumstances it is appropriate to tell others in the individual's environment about possible risks to themselves. The following short case illustrations help to identify the dilemmas.

CASE 1

'Paul' is in the community on conditional discharge from hospital (Sections 37/41 Hospital Order, Mental Health Act 1983). The order had been imposed for killing his wife. He had been detained in hospital for some ten years before being discharged by a Mental Health Review Tribunal. The facts of his original offence were that, having killed his wife (by manual strangulation), he had secreted her body and it was some months before it was discovered. At the time of his arrest he had been seeing another woman on a regular basis. A year after his conditional discharge he informed his supervising probation officer that he had been seeing a woman and hoped to marry her. The probation officer's responsibilities in this case seem clear. In the first instance, the development needs to be reported to the relevant Home Office Department (Mental Health Unit). Second, the officer needs to ascertain from 'Paul' more details of the new relationship. In this discussion Paul would need to be advised that he should inform the woman of his past history (given the particular circumstances of his original offence). Should 'Paul' refuse to do so, it is likely that the probation officer (having taken advice from his line management and maybe the Home Office) would inform 'Paul' that in the light of his refusal to do so, he would have to inform her himself. To some, this may seem like an intrusion into the offender–patient's personal liberty, but the broader issue of the protection of the public (in this case, the woman he is seeing) requires such action. It is this kind of intrusive intervention in the form of 'monitoring' that Walker (1991) suggests is crucial to work with such offenders. The issues of Case 1 seem fairly clear cut. In other cases there are grey areas that require careful consideration of who else should be involved; this is illustrated in Case 2.

CASE 2

This case situation arose before the current guidelines and instructions concerning the registration of some sex offenders (and paedophiles in particular) came into force.

'A' is a 60-year-old offender released on life licence for killing a child during a sexual assault. He has been living in the community on licence for about two years, and has so far given his probation officer no cause for concern. The probation officer has just received a phone call that 'A' has been seen 'loitering' by the bus stop outside a local primary school. What does the probation officer need to do about this development? There would appear to be several steps that need to be taken. First, further information is required as to the source and reliability of the information received. Did this information come via the school or, for example, from a bystander who knew 'A's history and was perhaps out to make trouble for him by deliberately misconstruing a quite innocent piece of behaviour? (He *could* have been waiting for a bus quite legitimately.) The second step in trying to elucidate the problematic behaviour would be to arrange a very urgent appointment to see 'A'. Why was he at this particular bus stop? His responses would have to be judged in the light of details about his original offence. It would be very ominous if he had picked up his original victim outside a school. Third, the supervising officer would have to consider the pros and cons of contacting the school and/or the local police to ascertain if any complaints or comments had been received concerning similar recent conduct by 'A'. Whatever steps the supervisor takes, *the offender is entitled to be told of the action proposed and the reasons for it.* Such information will be likely to be received and accepted more easily if 'A' was given very clear indications at the start of his life licence concerning his obligations under its terms. He needs to be made aware of the supervisor's responsibilities to report any apparently untoward conduct. Sadly, there have been occasions in the past when mutual expectations and obligations have not been shared openly. In such cases the offender can feel legitimately surprised when speedy and sometimes apparently condign action is taken. Some other aspects of the 'need to tell' are illustrated in the next case example.

CASE 3

A psychiatrist has been seeing regularly a male patient on an outpatient basis over a period of several months. In the past, he has had a number of compulsory admissions to hospital for a paranoid psychosis. During a recent session with his psychiatrist, he reveals a powerful belief that a former girl friend has been unfaithful to him, that he has been following her, and that he feels like killing her. What should the psychiatrist do? In the first instance he needs to check back over past records to see if similar beliefs have been expressed on other occasions and what the outcomes were. Second, he needs to make a careful appraisal of the quality of the patient's intended actions, discussing the case with other professionals and/or his professional body. For example, the circumstances of the self-reported stalking require careful and detailed evaluation, as does the quality of his expressed feelings about killing her. Feeling like killing someone is not quite the same as expressed threats to kill (which in law constitute a criminal offence). If his past history reveals similar threats and his *current* threats have a delusional intensity, then the psychiatrist would be exercising appropriate professional responsibility if he arranged for the patient's former girl friend to be warned about his feelings.[3]

From time to time one comes across cases in which the offender–patient has given clear indication of possible intended harm. In a recent inquiry in which I was involved (Prins et al., 1998), the perpetrator of a homicide (Sanjay Patel) who had been known to various health care and other agencies, gave a clear written warning to his supervising social worker of his possible intentions. He wrote in a letter from the prison in which he was then being held:

> I think that jail is the Best place for me at the moment because it sort's my head out. If I was on the street I would put peples life at risk, so that's over with (original spelling).

We commented as follows:

> Although in retrospect, everyone [now] considers that this letter was important and significant, at the time, its content and import was not communicated [by social services] to the Probation Service ... With hindsight, it would appear that the content of this letter might have prompted a referral for further psychiatric assessment.
> (Prins et al., 1998: 17)

We also found an escalating pattern of aggressive behaviour culminating in what should have been regarded as an ominous incident shortly before Patel killed his victim. He had been refused a grant from the Benefits Agency. He went to complain to the Social Services Department and the staff agreed to help him with an appeal. Not being satisfied with this he left the offices, and assaulted and demanded money from a stranger who was using the public telephone in the street outside the offices. The staff witnessed this behaviour but did not report it to the police; it was, however, reported to the Probation Service. The lesson to be derived from such varied incidents is that it is essential to chart them in order to determine whether or not a pattern of escalation is occurring. As a team, we considered that one of the key failings in this case was an inability to review events in this way. Some such persons will carry weapons, for example: Perry et al. (1998: 92) have drawn attention to the need to seek evidence of weapon carrying in patients. In a small study of a group of patients suffering from schizophrenia they found 'that a much greater number than expected carried weapons when unwell'. Failure to warn others can have disastrous consequences, as is demonstrated in the well-known case of Tarasoff.

CASE 4

Tarasoff v. *Regents of the University of California (1976)*   A young man named Poddar became infatuated with a female student named Tatiania Tarasoff. She rejected Poddar's overtures and, partly as a result of this rebuff, he went into psychotherapy with the university's counselling service. During this counselling Poddar is said to have revealed his intention to kill Tatiania and his plans to purchase a gun. Although the therapist tried to have Poddar detained (unsuccessfully in the event) no attempt was made to warn Tatiania or her family. Within two months Poddar had travelled to her home and killed her. Her family successfully sued the University of California for lack of duty of care. The Californian Supreme Court set a precedent in its ruling and legislation and other states followed suit: namely, that 'mental health professionals involved in the care of dangerous patients incurred a duty of care to warn *identifiable* third parties if, in the courses of the treatment of their patients, it became apparent that the said third parties were at risk from the patient' [emphasis added] (Turner & Kennedy, 1997: 465). It should be noted here that the duty to warn applied only to identifiable potential victims. Applebaum (1994: 77) summarises the Supreme Court's ruling in this way:

> That a therapist who 'determines, or pursuant to the standards of his profession should determine, that his patient presents a serious danger of violence to another' has a duty to take whatever steps are 'reasonably necessary' to protect the intended victim.

Such a ruling has not, so far, been tested in the UK courts, but the case of *W* v. *Egdell* has provided a clear indication that professionals may on occasion exercise their judgement in favour of public protection.

CASE 5

W v. Egdell (1989)   W was a detained Special Hospital patient, having been made subject to a Hospital Order with Restrictions (Sections 37/ 41, Mental Health Act 1983). His offences had consisted of several killings and woundings. Dr Egdell had been asked by W's solicitors to provide an independent psychiatric report for W's forthcoming Mental Health Review Tribunal. Egdell's report did not recommend either discharge or transfer to less secure conditions. W's solicitors did not present the report to the Tribunal. Egdell, concerned about W's continuing dangerousness, sent a copy of his report to the managers of the hospital who subsequently forwarded it to the Home Office. W subsequently brought an action against Egdell on the grounds of breach of confidentiality. The High Court ruled against W on the grounds that the public interest outweighed W's right to confidentiality. However, the Court gave clear indication that their ruling did not have a general application: confidentiality should be breached only if it was deemed necessary to protect the public interest; secondly the 'risk must be real rather than fanciful' and 'third the risk must involve danger of physical harm' (Turner & Kennedy, 1997: 466). In general terms, the obligations placed on mental health and allied professionals are somewhat unclear and until very recently there has been little decisive official guidance on the subject. However, under the terms of Section 115 of the Crime and Disorder Act 1998, there is established a *general* power to disclose information between the police and other public bodies 'for the prevention, detection and reduction of crime'. The *Introductory Guide* to the Act (Home Office, 1998a: 27) states that Section 115 'puts beyond doubt the power of any organisation to disclose information to police authorities, local authorities, probation committees, health authorities, or to persons acting on their behalf, so long as such disclosure is necessary or expedient for the purposes of this Act'. Although this provision seems to make disclosure more easy than in the past, it should be noted that such disclosure is for the purposes of *general* crime prevention and it is clear that such disclosures would not apply in some of the cases discussed above. Chapter 5 of the *Guidance* reinforces this cautionary note, as follows:

> 5.14   Although section 115 ensures that lawful powers are available to all agencies for the disclosure of information to relevant authorities for the purposes of the Act, the law of confidence still applies. This means that anyone proposing to disclose information

not publicly available and obtained in circumstances giving rise to a duty of confidence will need to establish whether there is an over-riding justification for doing so. If not, it is still necessary to obtain the informed consent of the person who supplied the information. This will need to be assessed on a case-by-case basis, and legal advice should be sought in any case of doubt.

(Home Office, 1998b: 5.14)

Thus, it can be seen that although there has been a sharpening of the guidance in terms of *general* crime prevention, cases at the individual level will still have to be decided on their merits. The recent large number of homicide and other inquiries, referred to in Chapter 4, may now have engendered an atmosphere in which decisions to impart information to third parties will be viewed more sympathetically and that future case law may well tend to favour such disclosure. Time alone will tell.

ASPECTS OF COMMUNICATION

As indicated in Chapter 4, very many inquiries into homicides and other incidents have catalogued failures in communication on a very large scale. We must now consider why this should be and what might be done to remedy the situation. A favourite quotation of mine is from John Wilson, not a mental health or criminal justice professional, but a commentator on English literature: 'All tragedy is the failure of communication' (Wilson, 1974: 9). It is the kind of aphorism that should be in the offices or workplaces of all such professionals. It is possible to expand on this arresting aphorism in four distinct ways.

First, there is the need for good professional inter-agency and inter-disciplinary communication. Case conferences have been in existence for many years and are thought by many to be useful mechanisms for the exchange of information and the formation of action plans. Much of our current mental health legislation and practice is based on this important device. Why is it then that so often they seem to be unproductive? In my view, part of the failure comes about because of an inability to distinguish between *inter-agency* and *interdisciplinary*. Let us consider a case conference at which are present a consultant psychiatrist, a clinical psychologist, a psychiatric nurse, a probation officer/or other social worker and a police officer. All these good people are trained in different ways and bring to such a conference certain assumptions and expectations about the roles they should play and the duties they should perform.

A psychiatrist is first of all a doctor; he or she has then taken a further lengthy training in psychiatry (which may involve further sub-specialisation in child/adolescent/forensic/adult psychiatry). His or her world view may well be coloured by the deference customarily paid to physicians – a deference that has become increasingly ambivalent in recent years. To understand this we should note that the first physicians were descended from the priests, and revered because of this. Currently, this reverence born of the 'magic' they can perform over us has been diluted by a growing tendency to wish to hold them accountable if they get things wrong. In addition, their role in psychiatric practice is exacerbated by legal issues. For example, under the Mental Health Act 1983 they are held to be the Responsible Medical Officer (RMO) and it is they who are held accountable in law if things go wrong. It is, therefore, hardly surprising that they may become impatient of what they may regard as the less than important views of others who do not have their long training and who do not bear legal responsibility. From time to time, such medical men and women have held others in scant regard and been criticised for failure to consult with or marginalising the contributions of others (see Blom-Cooper et al., 1996). A worrying example is to be found in the *Report into the care and treatment of Richard Stoker* (Brown et al., 1996). In this case, the RMO was criticised for failing to communicate with relevant colleagues, a failure that had led to serious concern. This had been a long-standing issue and 'one of considerable concern to the Trust' (p. 26). In fairness, it must be said that at the inquiry, the RMO acknowledged her failings: 'I am a person who prefers to do rather than write and I have no illusions about that' (p. 26). The authors of the *Report* state that 'There seems to us to have been an almost surprising forbearance shown to her shortcomings . . . because of the high regard in which she was held as a Clinical Psychiatrist and her clinical competence' (p. 26). However, the Chief Executive stated in his evidence to the inquiry that 'spending 100 per cent of her time with her patients was one thing but not letting the rest of the Care Team know what was happening was another thing because "if she did not get that balance right then she actually was not doing good to anybody"' (p. 26; see also Reith, 1998). In other words, one should never try to 'go it alone'.[4]

To return to our case conference: the clinical psychologist will have a general background in psychology before taking a further psychological specialism (such as clinical, educational or forensic psychology). He or she will bring to the task expertise in the use of specific assessment devices, and perhaps not have much regard for the more open-ended and vaguer methods of clinical assessment (such as in-depth interviewing).[5] Social workers have a variety of trainings. They come from a variety of backgrounds; some are young university entrants to the profession; others enter later in life after having had other employments. Currently, the profession is not as well controlled as medicine, nursing or psychology but, as a result of recent concerns about bad or indifferent practice, there are proposals to regulate the profession in similar fashion. A former Home Secretary took the view that a formal university training was not needed for work as a probation officer – an opinion that was, in my view, as dangerous as it was meretricious – and training was largely withdrawn from the university sector.

Psychiatric nurses (be they hospital or community based) have been playing an increasingly important role in psychiatry in recent years. From a somewhat defensive stance in the early days of the profession, psychiatric nursing has emerged as a discipline to be reckoned with and one which has become increasingly professionalised. Finally, police officers (who today tend increasingly to come from a variety of backgrounds) may be seen by others to over-represent the more coercive aspects of law and order. They work within a more clearly defined hierarchical structure than the other disciplines represented at the case conference. Those police officers with CID experience make excellent contributions to any debate about risk-taking, since the best of them combine realism with considerable sensitivity.

When one considers the differences I have referred to, it is hardly surprising that it can take many years of working together to achieve a way of reaching consensus that acknowledges these different perspectives, together with a degree of comfort to really say what one thinks!

The *second* aspect concerns the need for adequate communication between the worker (of whatever discipline) and the client (offender, offender–patient). This embraces a number of elements. Some high-risk offenders have committed not only very serious offences, but offences that involve extreme cruelty or perversion. Workers may not come across such individuals very frequently in their careers and may have very real feelings of revulsion and fear. Unless these elements are recognised and worked through (preferably through good professional supervision) they are likely to get in the way of effective therapeutic engagement.

However, some writers have asserted that a certain distancing is also required. P.D. James (1997: 276), in one of her recent crime novels, states:

> Like doctors, nurses or the traffic police who extract the pulped bodies from the crushed metal, you couldn't do the job if your thoughts were centred on your own emotions. It was necessary to grow a carapace, however fragile, of acceptance and detachment if one was to remain competent and sane. Horror might enter, but must never be allowed to make a permanent lodging in the mind.

This sense of necessary but empathic detachment is echoed by another novelist, G. O'Connor, who writes, 'Sometimes it appears, the unconscious solves problems more effectively than an overworked and cluttered brain' (O'Connor, 1998: 242). In his two excellent books on therapeutic engagement, Casement (1985; 1990) outlines ways in which, as a psychoanalytic psychotherapist, he learned to benefit from his mistakes through introspection. The phenomenon of denial is a well-recognised mechanism used by patients; it is less well recognised that workers may also engage in such denial (see later discussion). Workers of whatever discipline bring to their task a degree of what I have described in a previous work as 'ambivalent investment' (Prins, 1995a). It operates in the following three ways: (1) the worker may not have resolved earlier problems of having come to terms with the revulsion and fear referred to above. The result of this is to blind workers to the realities of the case and thus make them unable to take the necessary steps to overcome blockages in therapeutic engagement; (2) even if the worker has overcome this, he or she then has to face the fact that they carry a great burden of responsibility for the welfare of the offender/offender–patient on the one hand, and the community on the other (see earlier discussion); and (3) the worker in his or her role as counsellor has a considerable investment in seeing that things are going well. This is because most people enter the counselling and caring professions from a desire to offer a service of care and restoration to people with a variety of needs. This may lead to a degree of unrealistic optimism about the progress of a case and the need for intrusive supervision, or monitoring (see Walker, 1991). For these three reasons there is, therefore, an overall investment in things going well from the outset because of the initial hurdles that have had to be overcome. Thus, mental health and criminal justice professionals may not wish to hear the bad news – that perhaps things are not going quite so well. They may, for example, ignore the half-spoken messages to this effect from the offender's relatives or from offenders themselves. Failed appointments following long periods of regular attendance, sudden changes of employment, a sense of unease when talking to relatives or partners may all require further exploration before difficulties escalate into traumatic incident. The famous physician William Osler once said in a lecture, 'Listen to the patient; he is telling you the diagnosis'. This aphorism can usefully be applied to the forensic setting.

How can some of these pitfalls be avoided? One way is to maintain good written records and, more importantly, *consult them frequently*. We all suffer from the somewhat arrogant assumption that we can recall details of our counselling encounters adequately. This is not the case as we can soon discover if we look back at a series of interviews undertaken, say over a six-month period. Some of the missed opportunities and gaps in the accounts will emerge all too clearly. In addition, in these days of accountability and openness, it is very useful to engage the offender/offender–patient as much as possible in the record-keeping process. This sharing will not only engage him/her, but will serve as a benchmark for future reference. The sharing will also encourage the offender/offender–patient to feel that they, too, are making a real contribution to the therapeutic endeavour. To paraphrase: the price that supervisors pay for ensuring the liberty of the subject to live safely in the community is that of eternal vigilance. Supervisors must, therefore, be prepared to ask the kind of uncomfortable questions that I refer to in the final section of this chapter.

The *third* aspect of communication is to ask: how well do mental health and criminal justice professionals listen to the concerns of the non-professional carers of their charges? These will include spouses, partners, siblings and others close to the offender/offender–patient. In the inquiry into the Andrew Robinson case referred to in Chapter 4, the inquiry team was informed that Andrew's parents (who were very intelligent and articulate people) had attempted, over a period of time, to get the professionals engaged in Andrew's care to listen to their concerns about his continued psychotically motivated aggression towards them. For them, their home had become a place of terror (Blom-Cooper et al., 1995). In too large a number of some of the inquiries referred to in Chapter 4 similar instances have occurred. It seems that relatives are sometimes marginalised by the professionals, and this has sometimes resulted in tragic outcomes for all concerned. In fairness, one has to recognise that it is not always easy to engage relatives in the risk assessment/management process if the offender/offender–patient does not give consent for such engagement. However, it is becoming clear that in cases involving issues of public protection, consent may need to be overridden.

The *fourth* and final aspect to be considered has to some extent already been touched on, namely the need for the worker to be in touch with the warring parts of themselves. This involves, for example, a sensitive appreciation of race and gender issues. In the inquiry I chaired into the death of Orville Blackwood in Broadmoor we considered that although there was no evidence of active racist malpractice, there was evidence of a lack of sensitivity to the needs of ethnic minority groups, most notably African-Caribbeans. There was also a tendency to see such black patients as 'big, black and dangerous' because of their size and ethnic origins, where there was no evidence for such an assumption. To mark our concerns about this, we subtitled our report *Big, black and dangerous*, with a question mark added. Another disquieting feature to emerge was the absence of any ethnic minority representation, either on the senior management staff of the hospital, or on the then managing Health Authority (Prins et al., 1993). On a return visit (by invitation) to Broadmoor some four years after our inquiry, I found there was still sadly no such representation; I was also informed that the numbers of ethnic minority nursing staff had shown a *decrease*. There are other aspects to ethnic awareness that should be borne in mind. Practices that we Eurocentric professionals take for granted, such as the use of fore and surnames, require sensitive understanding, as does regard for the dietary requirements of some cultural groups. I cannot elaborate on these matters here, but Suman Fernando and other colleagues have written extensively and helpfully on these matters, and their work should be compulsory reading for all those engaged in work with ethnic minority patients/offenders/offender–patients.[6] Other areas of concern are gender issues, particularly in relation to serious sex offending. Male workers have not always been as perceptive as they might be to the manner in which rapists and other serious sexual transgressors perceive themselves. As with ethnic issues, publications in this area should be consulted in order to encourage a greater degree of sensitivity.[7]

Before considering the need to establish an effective baseline from which to operate, it is important to refer to a concept that is basic to risk assessment and management – namely that of *vulnerability*. This is concerned with taking as much care as possible not to return the offender/offender–patient to a situation in which the dangerous behaviour that led to the original offence or other matter can be readily re-enacted. One is mindful of the case of Graham Young, already referred to in this book. Sometimes one's best efforts not to do so are defeated by lack of adequate resources, such as housing appropriate to the individual's needs or lack of good hostel and day-care facilities. Nevertheless, from a strictly clinical point of view, one may sometimes ignore possible dangers. We might well pause to consider the words of Shakespeare's King John, contemplating the blinding of the young Prince Arthur he says: 'How oft the sight of means to do ill deeds makes deeds ill done' (*King John*, IV, ii). Proper regard for *both* the vulnerability of the public *and* the vulnerability of the offender/offender–patient may well prevent further incidents of violence and trauma for all concerned or, what the late Dr Murray Cox wisely called 'unfinished business' (Cox, 1979: 310).

ESTABLISHING AN EFFECTIVE BASELINE OR 'ACTING ON INFORMATION RECEIVED'

All the research and clinical studies in the field of risk assessment and management in mental health and criminal justice attest to the importance of the need to obtain the essential facts of the situation which have led to the need to assess risk to others. It is this kind of evidence that decision-making bodies, such as the Parole Board, the Home Secretary's Advisory Board on Restricted Cases and the Mental Health Review Tribunal require in order to make the most effective decisions (see also Chapter 2). This necessitates having an accurate and full record of, for example, the index offence or other incident and, in addition, the person's previous history, particularly their previous convictions. A bare legal description tells us nothing about seriousness of intention at the time of the offence, or its prognostic significance. This has become of increasing importance today, when plea bargaining in overstretched Crown Courts, and advocates' attempts to downgrade offences have become more frequent. An incident that may well have had the ingredients to justify an original charge of attempted murder may eventually end up, by agreement, as one of unlawful wounding (see, for example, Collier, 1995). Neither do the bare details of an offence give adequate insight into the role played by the victim in the offence. In an interesting contribution to the topic of victim-precipitated homicide, Polk (1997: 141) writes as follows:

> Despite the enduring popularity of the term, there are many problems in its use for the present-day study of homicide, including the lack of adequate details in files for the determination of the role of the victims for a large number of cases, as well as the fact that

inevitably, the various actors in a homicide scene have different views of what happened, so it may be difficult to establish the facts of the case (especially as the victim will not be present).

The bare details of an offence also give little real indication of motivation. For example, burglary may take the form of a conventional break-in, or it may have more significant prognostic implication, if, for example, the only items stolen were the shoes belonging to the female occupant of the premises, or if, accompanying the break-in, there was evidence of wilful damage such as the slashing of the bed-sheets in the main bedroom (see, for example, Morneau & Rockwell, 1980). In similar fashion, those males who expose themselves to women in an aggressive fashion associated with erection, masturbatory activity and sometimes orgasm, need to be distinguished from those who are more passive, are non-confrontational and who expose from a distance without erection (see Bluglass, 1980). Scott, in his seminal paper on *Assessing dangerousness in criminals*, stressed the need for a most careful scrutiny of the basic facts, and in doing so he showed that there is no magic to be brought to this task; just attention to detail:

> It is patience, thoroughness and persistence in this process [of data collection], rather than any diagnostic brilliance that produces results. In this sense, the telephone, the written request for past records and the checking of information against other informants, are the important diagnostic devices. Having collected the facts under the headings (1) the offence; (2) past behaviour; (3) personal data; (4) social circumstances, it is useful to scan them from a number of different directions with a view to answering certain key questions concerning dangerousness.
>
> (Scott, 1977: 129)

Scott was not of course the first to emphasise the importance of taking the thoughtful time-centred rounded view. Some eighty years earlier, Freud had stated: 'I learned to follow the unforgotten advice of my master Charcot: to look at the same things again and again, until they themselves began to speak' (Freud, 1914: 22). And in his book *Foucault's pendulum*, Eco asserts that 'no piece of information is superior to any other. Power lies in having them on file and then finding the connections; you only *want to have to find them*' (Eco, 1989: 225; emphasis added).

In addition to the written information about the offence or other deviant behaviour, it may be very important to draw upon other sources such as the 'scene of crime' reports and photographs of the victim(s). They may serve to remind the worker of the seriousness of the offence and may also prove useful in confronting attempts at denial by the offender during the course of therapeutic engagement. For example, the act of killing can involve a great deal of very real unpleasantness which may diminish in the workers' minds over time. In other words, the original offence may become devalued or downgraded as seemed to have happened in Andrew Robinson's case. Lady Macbeth exemplifies this phenomenon: having derided her husband for being 'infirm of purpose' in not smearing the sleeping grooms with blood to implicate them in the killing of King Duncan, she begins her descent into guilt-ridden madness, uttering when *in extremis*: 'Who would have thought the old man to have had so much blood in him?'

Modern writers have also demonstrated this need to obtain a complete view of the facts. For example, Ruth Rendell's Chief Inspector Wexford

> sat looking at the scene of crime photographs . . . the kind of pictures no one but himself would ever see, the results of real violence, real crime. Those great splashes and stains were real blood. Was he privileged to see them or unfortunate?
>
> (Rendell, 1992: 148)

Obviously Inspector Kate Miskin in P.D. James's *Original sin* also thought such proximity was important, since she says, 'Every victim dies because of who he is, what he is, where he is at one moment of time. The more you know about the victim, the closer you are to his murderer' (James, 1994: 344).

And the detective in Peter Ackroyd's novel *Hawksmoor* says;

> You can tell a great deal about the killer from the kind of death he inflicts; an eager person will kill in a hurried manner, a tentative person will do it more slowly . . . you must remember, too, the sequence of actions which follow the murder; most killers are stunned by their action. They sweat; sometimes they become very hungry and thirsty; many of them lose control of their bowels at the moment of death, just as their victims do . . . murderers will try to recall the sequence of events; they will remember exactly what they did just before and just after . . . but they can never remember the actual moment of killing. The murderer always forgets that, and that is why he will always leave a clue.
>
> (Ackroyd, 1985: 159)

In his account of his functions as a forensic psychologist and, in particular, his work as a profiler, Britton likens this need to assemble the pieces to working on a series of jigsaw puzzles. He says:

> It's like working on several jigsaw puzzles at one time. One puzzle will tell me that happened, another will reveal how it happened, a third will tell me about the victim and a fourth will show me the likely motivation of the offender. When completed, each of these puzzles then becomes a vital piece in a much larger jigsaw that will help me identify the psychological characteristics of the offender.
>
> (Britton, 1997: 145)[8]

A number of official and semi-official publications have appeared in recent years which offer guidance on risk assessment: for example, the Department of Health's *Guidance on the discharge of mentally disordered people and their continuing care in the community* (Department of Health, 1994). The advice emphasises the following points, among others, advocated by the panel of inquiry into the case of Kim Kirkman (West Midlands Regional Health Authority, 1991: 7):

> Past history of the patient; self-reporting by the patient at interview; observation of the behaviour and mental state of the patient; *discrepancies between what is reported and what is observed*; statistics derived from studies of related cases and prediction indicators derived from research [emphasis added].

Comparable points are made by the Association of Chief Officers of Probation (1994: 5) in their *Guidelines on the management of risk and public protection*. For example, they suggest such questions as:

> Who is likely to get hurt? How seriously and in what way? Is it likely to happen right now, next week or when? How often? In what circumstances will it be more rather than less likely to occur? Is the behaviour that led to the offending continuing? What is he/she telling you, not only by words but also by demeanour/actions?

The Mental Health Unit of the Home Office has produced a useful checklist of questions to be taken into account by those dealing with conditionally discharged restricted patients in the community. It is reproduced as Appendix I to this chapter; and see also Dent (1997).

IMPROVING PRACTICE

Risk registers and other protocols

I've got a little list

(Koko in *The Mikado*)

I have already made brief reference to registration as a tool in risk assessment and management. The notion of such registration has its advocates and its detractors. Those in favour consider that it will make it easier to attract funds to cases and make it easier to enable problematic cases to be tackled more effectively. Others have pointed to certain disadvantages: for example, additional stigma being attached to the severely mentally disordered and to the possibility of professionals being held legally accountable if they did *not* register a patient and that patient then committed a serious offence such as homicide. Writing on the use of registration in relation to *child abuse*, the Bridge Child Care Consultancy Service (who, as indicated in chapter 4 reported on certain aspects of the West case) stated:

> Procedures in themselves do not protect children if they are not considered to be at risk. We do not in this report therefore recommend any substantial change in procedures but *we do recommend* that the ACPC and its constituent members be wary of reducing their vigilance in dealing with suspicions of abuse.
>
> (Bridge Child Care Consultancy Service, 1995: 15)

This observation is capable of extrapolation to all instances where wariness is needed and where the mere fact that registration has taken place and 'something has been done' may blind us to the need for further action.[9] Most authorities now have elaborate protocols for the assessment and further management of risk. It should be noted that I use the term 'further management' immediately after the *assessment* of risk. This is because I consider the two processes should not be considered as separate entities, but as one seamless flowing endeavour. Probation Services have gone to considerable lengths to produce comprehensive protocols. Extracts from one of these devices are produced by kind permission of the Gloucestershire Probation Service as Appendix II to this chapter.

Asking the 'unimaginable', the 'unthinkable' and the 'unaskable'

Although there can be no prescriptions that can be set down for the effective supervision of high risk individuals, there are perhaps certain

areas which can and should be usefully explored by whoever is supervising them. As I have already indicated, this type of work requires a
certain degree of introspective activity on the part of the worker, and a
capacity to deal with one's blind spots and personal anxieties. In addition, those responsible for the day-to-day supervision of such persons
deserve not only the support and supervision of their line managers, but
also the recognition that such work is highly demanding in terms of
time, energy and emotions. Thus, due allowance should be made for
this in the allocation of case-loads. Time should also be allowed for
further professional development and for keeping up with the literature
relating to the worker's particular discipline.

In a previous work (Prins, 1995a) I briefly suggested a number of
relevant areas of questioning. I have now developed these further, as
follows:

1   Have those stresses and precipitants that appear to have conduced
    to the offender/offender–patient's past offending or other problem-
    atic behaviour been dealt with to the extent that it now seems
    acceptable to release/discharge them into the community? If reso-
    lution is not complete (can it ever be?) has there been enough to
    still make the risk tolerable? If so, is the nature of the services and
    supervision required likely to be equal to the task? As already
    stated, this may be dependent as much on the availability of
    adequate material resources as it is upon the skills of the supervisors.
    So much has been written in recent years about risk in its various
    forms (but most notably in the spheres of mental health care and
    criminal justice) that many workers must have felt increasingly
    deskilled and formed the view that only very sophisticated psycho-
    social methods of practice will serve. The aim of this book is to
    suggest that there is no magic or philosopher's stone in this area of
    work. I would refer readers again to the late Dr Peter Scott's paper
    on this subject, since he did more than most of us to help to
    demystify the risk management process (Scott, 1977).

2   The next point to be considered is really an extension of the ques-
    tions posed above; however, its importance merits consideration in
    its own right. The question to be answered is: What is this indi-
    vidual's capacity to deal with provocation? Have reactions to past
    provoking incidents been examined and confronted by the offender/
    offender–patient? It is well known that violent feelings and actions
    may be displaced from their original source on to an innocent
    victim as, for example, in the killing of the innocent stranger in the

street. In the Patel inquiry already referred to, we did not consider our remit extended to an examination of Sanjay's motives for the killing of his unknown victim. However, it will be vital for those having his future management to try to ascertain in some detail what led him to kill an innocent stranger. Using a literary allusion, we may well wonder why it was that the innocent Polonius fell victim to Hamlet's homicidal behaviour. Who *was* Hamlet intent on killing? Careful scanning (in Scott's terms) of the immediate environment may enable us to sense (and perhaps help the individual to avoid) potentially inflammatory situations. For example, to what extent has the over-flirtatious wife or partner of a jealous husband/partner courted a potentially dangerous situation by sarcasm, making denigrating remarks about sexual prowess, been otherwise contemptuous, or worn provocative clothing? The same is, of course, true with the male in the provocative role, as is the case from time to time in male homosexual relationships. Detailed accounts of previous provoking incidents are therefore vital in order to assess future risk and provide effective continuing management.

3   To what extent was the offence or other deviant behaviour person specific? Was it directed towards a particular individual for a specific purpose, or was it a means of getting back at society in general as, for example, with some arsonists? Such persons are, like the Monster (Victor) in Mary Shelley's *Frankenstein*, 'malicious because [they] are miserable'. Or, as expressed in the Book of Isaiah, do they feel 'despised and rejected of men'? Is this individual someone who still feels threatened or persecuted? Is this a personality trait developed in relation to some past experience or the result of ongoing mental illness which may yet be amenable to further modification or alleviation with the use of carefully monitored medication? Such success will, of course, depend on the degree of compliance on the part of the offender–patient and how effective our resources and methods are for securing it. Perception of the situation may be clouded by our tendency to place people and their disorders into watertight compartments; for example, one may have a serious disorder of personality (such as legally defined psychopathy) *and* develop a mental illness (such as a functional psychosis). Disorders are not mutually exclusive (see Chapter 3). It is well known that some individuals harbour feelings of rage and hatred for very long periods of time before they explode with catastrophic results (as, for example, in the case of Thomas Hamilton referred to in the last chapter). The sad thing is that these feelings so often do not emerge

before the catastrophic event and the person harbouring them may, more often than not, be perceived merely as rather sad loners (as in the case of Michael Ryan, the Hungerford multiple killer).

4   What clues are there concerning the offender/offender–patient's self image? This is of particular importance in relation to serious sex offenders such as rapists. It seems that past experiences may have contributed to their need to display a macho image that so often cruelly overrides the feelings, wishes and rights of their female victims.

5   How much continuing regard has been paid to what the offender– patient actually did at the time of the offence? Was the latter so horrendous that they blotted it out of consciousness? For example, did they wander off in a semi-amnesic state or, on realising what they had done, summon help immediately? Or, having mutilated the body before or after death, did they go off for a meal and/or a good night's sleep? How much are they still claiming the crime was sudden and spontaneous when the evidence shows careful planning and premeditation? What was the role of substance abuse of one kind or another? In the case of alcohol (which is usually regarded in law as an exacerbating rather than a mitigating factor) Rix (1989: 100) has proposed a useful distinction between alcohol *intoxication* and *drunkenness*. He proposes that:

> (1) the term 'alcohol intoxication' should refer to a state in which alcohol is present in the body; (2) its diagnosis should be based on toxicological evidence for the presence of alcohol in body fluids or tissues; and (3) the term 'drunkenness' should be used to describe behaviour displayed by people who have consumed, believe they have consumed, or want others to believe they have consumed, alcohol.

Prisons, and to a lesser extent secure hospitals, are not the ideal places for testing out future proclivities in such people. However, escorted periods of leave with close supervision may enable alcohol intake, for example, and its effects to be assessed. In similar fashion, the persistent paedophile on an escorted group outing to the seaside, in the company of other non-paedophile patients, may alert observant nursing staff to continuing abnormal sexual interest by having eyes only for the children playing on the beach. In similar fashion, nursing staff may report patients' continuing interest and arousal when in the presence of child visitors to the ward, or to pictures of children on the television. How much is known about what aids to sexual fantasies they are keeping in their rooms or cells? The offender/offender–patient who says he is writing his life history in a series of exercise books may usefully be asked to show them to us; somewhat surprisingly, they are often very willing to do so. We may find detailed descriptions of continuing violent and/or sadistic fantasies, which are being used as rehearsal for future activity. The case of Graham Young referred to earlier in this book is a good case in point. Another more recent example is the reported case of Colin Hatch – a parolee from a prison sentence – who choked to death a boy of seven. It was alleged at his trial that Hatch (who had previous convictions for sexual offences against young boys) had written down detailed sexual fantasies as to his intentions. Following his arrest, it was alleged that descriptions of some of these were found secreted in a wardrobe. 'They described in detail a fantasy where he tempted a 10-year-old girl to his room, stripped, raped, strangled and finally dumped her body in two bin liners.' Counsel for the prosecution stated 'His writing included references to deliberate killing . . . in the fantasy story lack of consent is part of the story, that's part of the excitement. Killing and disposing of the body was part of the plan' (*Independent*, 18 January 1994: 2; 20 January 1994: 3). All such indicators, coupled with the use of psycho-physiological measuring devices, such as penile plethysmography (measurement of sexual arousal under laboratory conditions) may help us to obtain a better, if not conclusive, perception of likely future behaviour. However, it should be remembered that fantasies are not always acted upon. It is when they are, or have been, associated with actual *behaviour*, that concerns should be raised in serious fashion.

6   To what extent has the offender/offender–patient come to terms with what they did and been able to confront their offending behaviour? In the past, experience has suggested that some offenders and offender–patients detained for many years have not had this issue addressed until release/discharge is being considered. The lapse of many years without intervention can be a serious stumbling block to risk assessment and future management.

Reference has already been made to the mechanism of *denial*. This must now be considered in more detail. In relation to paedophilic offenders and offender–patients, Mezey and colleagues (1991) suggested that there were *six aspects of denial* that were of importance. I have paraphrased them briefly as follows:

1   Denial of the act itself. Such denial will be exemplified by denial of the offence behaviour to the police, prosecution service, courts and those charged with their subsequent containment and management.
2   Denial of the child's rights as a person, seeing the child as an object only.
3   Denial of the child as a victim. Paedophiles tend to see *themselves* as victims and the child as the instigator or willing participant, denying that there might be an unwillingness on the part of the child. (One can discern here similarities with rapists who refuse to accept that 'no' *means* 'no'.) Paedophiles cannot accept the fact that they are in a position of power and acknowledge the child's fear.
4   Denial of responsibility as an adult. They will indulge in such ploys as blaming the mother, spouse or partner. In some cases, their own histories of being sexually abused enable them to engage in this kind of denial that much more easily.
5   Denial of the consequences of their actions on the child.
6   Once in treatment, they may feel that they have paid the price and be reluctant to admit their continuing interest in children. One member of the group described by Mezey et al. (1991: 18) said 'a future without children simply wasn't a future worth living'.

One of the most difficult problems is to try to determine how much insight the offender/offender–patient has developed into his or her offending. It is often the task of the professional to help these individuals face feelings and experiences that hitherto have been intolerable. We can only do this if we open ourselves to their troubled, terrified and terrifying worlds. It *may* be an ominous sign if the offender/offender–patient talks about his or her offence in an *apparently* guilt-free and callous manner. As counsellors we tend, for the reasons stated earlier in this chapter, to hope for protestations of guilt and/or remorse; we may be disquieted when these are not forthcoming in full measure. In this connection, Russel and Russel provide us with a useful caution-ary note:

> A person who expresses guilt is to be regarded with vigilance. His next move may be to engineer a situation where he can repeat his activities (about which he expresses guilt), but this time with rationalisation and hence without guilt. He will therefore try to manipulate his victim into giving him a pretext.
>
> (Russel & Russel, 1961: 38)

Wiest (1981) suggests that offenders or offender–patients tend to go through five stages in working through their guilt and remorse for what they have done (but not necessarily in the sequence given here). The first is *confession*: 'I take responsibility, and that's an end of it'. If I own up, 'all will be forgiven'. The second is *acceptance* of punishment; for example, being institutionalised for a long period of time is seen as meaning that nothing more needs to be done by the individual to work on their problems. The third phase is *denial* (which may operate at any time): 'It's all over, I can't undo it, life must go on'. The fourth is the *grieving* state, grief for themselves and/or the victim. The fifth state is that of *remorse* which, as the poet Emily Dickinson once said, is 'Memory – awake' (Wiest, 1981: 280). Care is needed in handling these issues since one can be easily misled. For example, a paedophile may dwell obsessively on how 'The children's lives have been ruined – they will never be normal themselves when they grow up – they will never recover from the experience'. These feelings may, of course, be genuine, but the preoccupation may indicate an ongoing 'molestation' in the offender's imagination (see earlier discussion of the role of fantasy and the cautionary note sounded by Russel & Russel, 1961, above).

Denial can, of course, operate for other reasons. Sometimes an offender or offender–patient may be reluctant to admit the truth of what they have done for fear of causing hurt to relatives and close others. McGrath (1989: 427) cites the case of the paedophilic sadistic killer who consistently denied his guilt in order to spare his 'gentle devoted parents who could not believe his guilt. When they died, within a fairly short while of each other, he willingly admitted his guilt, and in due course was released' (McGrath, 1989: 427). Sometimes – for example, in life sentence cases – denial of guilt makes release problematic. However, the High Court has held that 'a prisoner should not normally be refused parole *solely* because he/she does not admit he/she is guilty of the offence. The relevance of refusal to admit guilt depends on the circumstance of the case' (Stone, 1997: 124). Stone quotes the judgment of Lord Justice Stuart-Smith in the case of *R.* v. *Secretary of State and the Parole Board ex parte Zulfikar* [1995] (*The Times* Law Reports, 26 July: 10):

> At the end of the scale is the persistent offender, in particular the persistent sexual offender, who refuses to accept his guilt in the face of clear evidence and is unable to accept that he has a propensity to such conduct which needs to be tackled if he is not to offend again. At the other end of the scale is the first offender where the

motivation for the offence is clear and does not point to the likelihood of re-offending. In the majority of cases, whether or not the prisoner admits his guilt is unlikely to be more than one of many factors, to which undue weight should not be given.

(Quoted in Stone, 1997: 124/5; and personal communications 11 January and 10 February 1997)

Nor should we forget that an offender or offender–patient may be genuinely not guilty of the crime – as witnessed in a number of cases involving miscarriages of justice, such as the cases of the alleged killers of Maxwell Confait, the homicide allegation against the late Steven Kiszko and some terrorist cases.

The worker's feelings

These have already been touched on, but a few further and concluding observations are needed. Often the worker has to rely, at least initially, on his/her hunches. However, these need testing out: thus Commander Dalgleish in P.D. James's *Original sin* describes his 'instinct [as something] which he sometimes distrusted, but had learned not to ignore' (James, 1994: 268); and Sir Graham Smith, HM Chief Inspector of Probation, writing of his days as a probation officer dealing with high risk offenders, said: 'I learned to trust my instincts (if a person frightened me he was *probably* dangerous) and to go with that knowledge until I had analysed it for what it was worth' (Smith, 1995: 53; emphasis added).

I am always reminded of the second witch in *Macbeth* when she says 'By the pricking of my thumbs, something wicked this way comes' (IV, i). Can we be any more precise about what we are afraid of? We are all afraid of being the subject of physical violence, but it is useful to remember that some dangerous or potentially dangerous people may not only wish to be controlled but are, in addition, afraid of their own dangerous impulses. With such individuals it can be helpful to bring this out into the open; some such offenders and offender–patients may be afraid to talk about their feelings or fantasies because they feel the worker may be too frightened to listen to them. We cannot get it right every time and it would be foolish to think that we could. Holloway (1997: 284) puts it well when he says:

The very worst clinical practice does not involve making wrong decisions (however these might be defined), but the failure to make any decisions at all. Good practice requires decision making that has a rationale, clear-cut expectation of outcome, and provision for a change in the treatment plan if the expected outcome does not occur.

In this chapter my emphasis has been on matters of practical concern. In this respect it cannot be stressed enough that a most careful and chronological review of the offender or offender–patient's total experiences and the impressions gained about these by a *variety of observers* are crucial. And finally, five points need to be reiterated: *first*, the multifactorial and multi-disciplinary nature of the task; *second* the need for a disciplined and painstaking approach; *third*, the need for adequate and open communication between disciplines; *fourth*, a recognition of, and a capacity to accept, the need for a high level of surveillance in this particular type of work; *fifth* (and perhaps the most difficult), the need to develop a capacity to understand our own anxieties and blind spots. Let Shakespeare, with his usual insight, have the last word for professionals and their charges alike:

> And when we have our naked frailties hid,
> That suffer in exposure, let us meet,
> And question this most bloody piece of work
> To know it further.
>
> (*Macbeth*, II, iii)

APPENDIX I

Checklist of points considered by the home office in examining the cases of restricted patients

The role of the Home Office in the management of restricted patients is to protect the public from serious harm. To carry this out effectively, the Home Office needs to know:

(i) why a patient has been dangerous in the past;
(ii) whether they are still dangerous (if so, why; if not, why not and in what circumstances they might be dangerous again); and
(iii) what the treatment plan is.

The following list is not exhaustive, but is intended to cover some of the points which may need to be addressed when reporting to the Home Office. Not all points will apply to all patients; but all sections (not just that covering the main diagnosis) that apply to a particular patient should be completed. Attaching relevant reports is always encouraged.

Reports to the Home Office should reflect the views of the multi-disciplinary team. Please indicate whether the team has been consulted.

For all patients

1 Should the patient still be detained and for what reasons?
2 If yes, which level of security does the patient need?
3 What is the team's current understanding of the factors underpinning the index offence and previous dangerous behaviour?
4 What change has taken place in respect of those factors (i.e. to affect the perceived level of dangerousness)?
5 What are the potential risk factors in the future (e.g. compliance with medication, substance abuse, potential future circumstances, etc.)?
6 What are the patient's current attitudes to the index offence, other dangerous behaviour and any previous victims?
7 What is the outward evidence of change (i.e. behaviour in hospital, on leave, attitudes towards staff and patients and potential victim groups)? How has the patient responded to stressful situations? Describe any physical violence or verbal aggression.
8 Have alcohol or illicit drugs affected the patient in the past and did either contribute to the offending behaviour? If so, is this still a problem in hospital and what are the patient's current attitudes to drugs and alcohol? What specific therapeutic approaches have there been towards substance abuse?
9 Which issues still need to be addressed, and what are the short- and long-term treatment plans?
10 What is known about circumstances of the victim, or victim's family?

Patients with mental illness

11 How is the patient's dangerous behaviour related to their mental illness?
12 Which symptoms of mental illness remain?
13 Has stability been maintained under differing circumstances? Under what circumstances might stability be threatened?

14 Has medication helped and how important is it in maintaining the patient's stability?
15 To what extent does the patient have insight into their illness and the need for medication?
16 Does the patient comply with medication in hospital? Is there any reluctance? Would they be likely to comply outside?

Patients with psychopathy

17 What are the individual characteristics of the personality disorder?
18 What have been the treatment approaches to specific problem areas?
19 Is the patient now more mature, predictable and concerned about others? Please give evidence.
20 Are they more tolerant of frustration and stress? Please give evidence.
21 Does the patient now take into account the consequences of their actions and learn from experience? Please give evidence.

Patients with mental impairment

22 How has the patient benefited from treatment/training?
23 Is their behaviour more acceptable? Please give evidence.
24 Is the patient's behaviour explosive or impulsive? Please give evidence.
25 Does the patient now learn from experience and take into account the consequences of their actions? Please give evidence.

Patients with dangerous sexual behaviour (all forms of mental disorder)

26 Does the patient still show undesirable interest in the victim type?
27 Describe any access to the victim type and the patient's attitude towards this group?
28 What form has sexual activity in hospital taken?
29 What do psychological tests or other evaluation indicate?
30 What is the current content of fantasy material?

Patients who set fires (all forms of mental disorder)

31 What interest does the patient still have in fires?
32 Have they set fires in hospital?
33 What access do they have to a lighter or matches?

34 In what way do fires appear in current fantasy material?
35 Does the patient have insight into previous fire setting behaviour?

And, finally

36 Please give any other relevant information which would be useful to the Home Office.

APPENDIX II

Gloucestershire probation service

NAME OF OFFENDER:...............................
CHECKLIST TO ASSIST RISK ASSESSMENT

This guidance is in the form of a checklist and questions and is intended to assist in the risk assessment process. It may highlight the need for more information to be obtained. Feelings and hunches must be taken into account but try to put words to them.

1 Information Available

PSR (Pre-Sentence Report)	
CPS (Crown Prosecution Service)	
Previous convictions	
Psychiatrist reports(s)	
Psychologist report(s)	
Post-sentence reports (lifers)	
Parole reports	
Summary of offences	

2 Offence(s): current/previous

Have you got full details/circumstances/motivation/attitude?

		Current	*Prev.*
1	Murder/Manslaughter		
2	Rape		
3	Arson/Criminal Damage Endangering Life		
4	Wounding		
5	Use/Possession of Firearms/Weapons		
6	False Imprisonment/Kidnapping		
7	Any offence against Children		
8	Indecent Assault		
9	Indecent Exposure		
10	Robbery		
11	Aggravated Burglary		
12	Serious drug offences		
13	Dangerous Driving		
14	Other serious offence (please specify)		
	No such offences known		
	Full list of Previous Convictions not seen		

3   History

		Yes/No
1	Ever sentenced to 4 years or more	
2	Sentenced as Young Person under Section 53 of CYPA 1993	
3	Ever subject to Conditional Discharge from Special Hospital	
4	More than one conviction for violent offence	
5	Any previous assault against Probation or other public service staff	
6	Any previous threats against Probation or other public service staff	
7	Any previous sexual advances against Probation or other staff	
8	History of suicide attempts or other self-harm	
9	Other (please specify)	
	None of above known	

4   Victim Details (current/previous offences)

		Current	Prev.
1	Known to the perpetrator		
2	Stranger		
3	Pre-meditated		
4	Impulsive		
5	Victim targeted		
6	Sex of victim(s)		
7	Age of victims(s)		
8	Membership of particular group		
9	Weapon used		
10	Weapon carried		
11	Violence threatened		
12	Violence carried out		

5   Child Related Concerns

1	Survivor of abuse or neglect as a child	
2	Aged 20 or less and a parent	
3	Lone parent	
4	Step-parent	
5	Socially isolated/frequent moves/ poor housing	
6	Subject to poverty	
7	Educational difficulty	
8	Substance abuser	
9	Any history or involvement in abuse or neglect	
10	Ever subject to Child Protection procedure or enquiry	
11	In contact with child(ren) on Child Protection Register	
12	History of domestic violence	
13	Other factors (please specify)	
	None of the above apparent	

6   Present Circumstances/Behaviour

1	Alcohol/drug/solvents/substance abuse	
2	Socially isolated or 'alienated lifestyle'	
3	Indications of mental disorder or obsessional behaviour	
4	Expression of hostility/resentment/anti-authority feelings	
5	Inappropriate sexual behaviour or advances	
6	Intolerance/frustration/inability to feel sympathy for others	
7	No evidence of victim empathy	
8	Other (please specify)	
	None of above apparent	

7   Specific questions to be answered

1	Who is likely to get hurt?	
2	How seriously and in what way?	
3	Is it likely to happen right now, next week, or when?	

4	How often?
5	In what circumstances will it be more, rather than less, likely to occur?
6	What is the worst the individual has ever done, and in what circumstances?
7	Is the behaviour that led to the offending continuing?
8	What are the patterns of behaviour?
9	What has previously stopped him/her?
10	Does he/she want to be stopped? In what way has this been demonstrated?
11	What is he/she saying about the victim(s)?
12	What has been the impact to date of the work undertaken?
13	What is the client saying about likely actions?

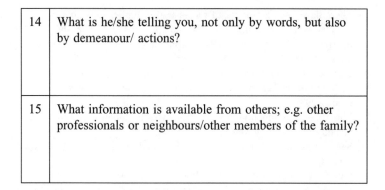

14	What is he/she telling you, not only by words, but also by demeanour/ actions?
15	What information is available from others; e.g. other professionals or neighbours/other members of the family?

Readers should note that this checklist forms but a *very small part* of a very comprehensive document, which covers such aspects as: risk management policy; procedures; disclosure; multi-agency practice regarding *mentally disordered* offenders; and expectations of duties to be performed by supervising staff, line management and the Probation Board (Committee).

NOTES

1 The need to remember the force of media pressure has already been referred to in earlier parts of this book. They have been well addressed recently by Soothill and Francis (1997) in the context of scaremongering concerning sex offenders, notably paedophiles.

2 See in particular their work on a violence prediction scheme (Webster et al., 1994). For a discussion of the problems in predicting prisoners' day-to-day behaviour within the prison environment, see Munro and Macpherson (1998).

3 Psychiatrists and other medical practitioners not infrequently find themselves in situations where there are other ethical dilemmas in relation to legal requirements. A good example is that of fitness to drive a motor vehicle. In a small-scale survey, Thompson and Nelson (1996) found that many psychiatrists were unaware of the regulations concerning certification for fitness to drive. In an earlier reported survey, Lowrie and Milne (1994) found that, of patients on the acute wards of a psychiatric hospital, roughly 40 per cent held driving licences, the majority of whom would be affected by the current regulations concerning fitness for driving. Few of the patients interviewed recalled ever having been given advice on the regulations concerning driving. A number of such patients would have presented grave hazards if they had been driving when unwell. It seems that patients and psychiatrists alike seemed unaware of the regulations governing such risky behaviour.

4 There have been a number of recent useful publications on various aspects
   of inter-agency working; see, for example: Home Office and Department
   of Health (1995); Petch (1996); Department of Health (1996); Department of Health (1997); Department of Health (1998); Reith (1998). An
   example of failures in communication between a variety of agencies may
   be found in the report into a homicide committed by a service user (Dixon
   et al., 1997).
5 The roles and functions of psychologists in forensic settings have been
   recently reviewed by MacPherson (1997).
6 See, for example, Fernando (1995); Fernando et al. (1998); Littlewood and
   Lipsedge (1989); Bhui and Olajide (1999).
7 See, for example, Birch (1993); Radford and Russell (1992).
8 For additional accounts of the pros and cons of offender profiling, see Jackson
   and Bekerian (1997); and Holmes and Holmes (1996).
9 For further discussion of aspects of the history and controversies concerning
   risk registration, see Prins (1995b). For discussion on other aspects of care
   in the community, such as the care programme approach and supervised
   discharge, see Roy (1997).

REFERENCES

Legal cases cited

R. v. *Secretary of State and the Parole Board ex parte Zulfikar* [1995] *The
Times* Law Reports, 26 July: 10.
Tarasoff v. *Regents of the University of California* [1976] 2d. 334.
W. v. *Egdell* [1989] 1 ALL ER 1089.

Text references

Ackroyd, P. (1985). *Hawksmoor*. London: Sphere Books.
Applebaum, P.S. (1994). *Almost a revolution: Mental health law and the limits
of change*. Oxford: Oxford University Press.
Association of Chief Officers of Probation. (1994). *Guidelines on the manage-
ment of risk and public protection*. London: Author.
Bhui, K., & Olajide, D. (1999). *Mental health service provision for a multi-
cultural society*. London: Saunders.
Birch, H. (ed.). (1993). *Moving targets: Women, murder and representation*.
London: Virago.
Blom-Cooper, L. QC, Hally, H., & Murphy, E. (1995). *The falling shadow:
One patient's mental health care: 1978–1993*. London: Duckworth.
Blom-Cooper, L. QC, Grounds, A., Guinan, P., Parker, A., & Taylor, M. (1996).
The case of Jason Mitchell: Report of the independent panel of inquiry.
London: Duckworth.

Bluglass, R. (1980). Indecent exposure in the West Midlands. In D.J. West (ed.), *Sex offenders in the criminal justice system*. Cambridge: Institute of Criminology.

Bridge Child Care Consultancy Service. (1995). *Report prepared for Gloucestershire Area Child Protection Committee, Part 1: Case review: Overview Report in Respect of Charmaine and Heather West*. Gloucester: Gloucester County Council Social Services Department.

Britton, P. (1997). *The jigsaw man*. London: Corgi Books.

Brown, A.G., Harrop, F.M., Cronin, H.J., & Harman, J.C. (1996). *Report to the Northumberland Health Authority of the independent inquiry team into the care and treatment of Richard Stoker*. Northumberland: Northumberland Health Authority.

Carson, D. (1995). From risk assessment to risk management. In J. Braggins & C. Martin (eds), *Managing risk: Achieving the possible*. London: Institute for the Study and Treatment of Delinquency.

Casement, P. (1985). *On learning from the patient*. London: Tavistock.

Casement, P. (1990). *Further learning from the patient: The analytic space and process*. London: Tavistock/Routledge.

Collier, P. (1995). Wounding/assault offences: From prosecution to conviction. *Home Office Research Bulletin*, 37, 67–70.

Cox, M. (1979). Dynamic psychotherapy with sex offenders. In I. Rosen (ed.), *Sexual deviation* (2nd ed.). Oxford: Oxford University Press.

Crighton, D. (1999). Risk assessment in forensic mental health. *British Journal of Forensic Practice*, 1, 18–26.

Dent, S. (1997). The Home Office mental health unit and its approach to the assessment and management of risk. *International Review of Psychiatry*, 9, 265–71.

Department of Health. (1994). *Guidance on the discharge of mentally disordered people and their continuing care in the community* (HSG/94/27). London: Author.

Department of Health. (1996). *The health of the nation: Building bridges: A guide to arrangements for inter-agency working for the care and protection of severely mentally ill people*. London: Author.

Department of Health. (1997). *Developing partnerships in mental health*. London: Author.

Department of Health. (1998). *Probation and health: A guidance document aimed at promoting effective working between the Health and Probation Services*. London: Author.

Dixon, K., Gulliver, A., Reed, J., Rhys, M., & Mackay, J. (1997). *Report of the independent inquiry team following a homicide committed by a service user in April, 1996*. London: Bromley Health Authority, South East London Probation Service, London Borough of Bromley Social Services and Housing.

Dowie, J. (1990). Clinical decision making: Risk is a dangerous word and hubris is a sin'. In D. Carson (ed.), *Risk taking in mental disorder: Analyses, policies and practice strategies*. Chichester: SLE Publications.

Eco, U. (1989). *Foucault's pendulum*. London: Secker and Warburg.

Fernando, S. (ed.). (1995). *Mental health in a multi-ethnic society: A multi-disciplinary handbook*. London: Routledge.

Fernando, S., Ndegwa, D., & Wilson, M. (1998). *Forensic psychiatry, race and culture*. London: Routledge.

Freud, S. (1914). *On the history of the psychoanalytic movement* (Standard ed., Vol. 14). London: Hogarth Press and the Institute of Psycho-Analysis.

Greenland, C. (1980). Psychiatry and the prediction of dangerousness. *Journal of Psychiatric Treatment and Evaluation, 2*, 97–103.

Grounds, A. (1995). Risk assessment and management in clinical context. In J. Crichton (ed.), *Psychiatric patient violence: Risk and relapse*. London: Duckworth.

Gunn, J. (1990). Let's get serious about dangerousness. *Criminal Behaviour and Mental Health* (Supp.), 51–64.

Holloway, F. (1997). The assessment and management of risk in psychiatry: Can we do better? *Psychiatric Bulletin, 21*, 283–5.

Holmes, R.M., & Holmes, S.T. (1996). *Profiling violent crimes: An investigative tool* (2nd ed.). London: Sage.

Home Office & Department of Health. (1995). *Mentally disordered offenders: Inter-agency working*. London: Author.

Home Office. (1998a). *Crime and Disorder Act 1998: Introductory guide*. London: Author.

Home Office. (1998b). *Guidance on statutory crime and disorder partnerships: Crime and Disorder Act 1998*. London: Author.

Jackson, J.L., & Bekerian, D.A. (eds). (1997). *Offender profiling: Theory, research and practice*. Chichester: Wiley.

James, P.D. (1994). *Original sin*. London: Faber.

James, P.D. (1997). *A certain justice*. London: Faber.

Kemshall, H. (1996). Risk assessment: Fuzzy thinking and decisions in action? *Probation Journal, 43*, 2–7.

Kemshall, H. (1999). Risk assessment and risk management: Practice and Policy. *British Journal of Forensic Practice, 1*, 27–36.

Kvaraceus, W. (1966). *Anxious youth*. Columbus, Ohio: Columbus Press.

Littlewood, R., & Lipsedge, M. (1989). *Aliens and alienists: Ethnic minorities and psychiatry* (2nd ed.). London: Unwin Hyman.

Lowrie, D., & Milne, H. (1994). Mental disorder and driving. *Psychiatric Bulletin, 18*, 214–16.

Macpherson, G.J. (1997). Psychology and risk assessment. *British Journal of Clinical Psychology, 36*, 643–5.

McGrath, P. (1989). Book review. *British Journal of Psychiatry, 154*, 427.

Mezey, G., Vizzard, E., Hawkes, C., & Austin, R. (1991). A community treatment programme for convicted child sex offenders: A preliminary report. *Journal of Forensic Psychiatry, 2*, 11–25.

Morneau, R.H., & Rockwell, B.S. (1980). *Sex, motivation and the criminal offender*. Springfield, Ill.: Charles C. Thomas.

Munro, M., & Macpherson, G.J. (1998). Risk assessment: development of the OBS. *Forensic Up-Date*, *53*, 9–15.

O'Connor, G. (1998). *Farewell to the flesh*. London: Bantam Books.

Perry, D.W., Cormack, I.D., Campbell, C., & Reed, A. (1998). Weapon carrying: An important part of risk assessment. *Psychiatric Bulletin*, *22*, 281–3.

Petch, E. (1996). Mentally disordered offenders: Inter-agency working. *Journal of Forensic Psychiatry*, *7*, 376–82.

Polk, K. (1997). A re-examination of the concept of victim-precipitated homicide. *Homicide Studies*, *1*, 141–68.

Pollock, N., & Webster, C. (1991). The clinical assessment of dangerousness. In R. Bluglass, & P. Bowden (eds), *Principles and practice of forensic psychiatry*. London: Churchill Livingstone.

Prins, H. (1995a). *Offenders, deviants or patients* (2nd ed.). London: Routledge.

Prins, H. (1995b). I've got a little list' (Koko: *Mikado*) but is it any use? Comments on the forensic aspects of supervision registers for the mentally ill. *Medicine, Science and the Law*, *35*, 218–24.

Prins, H., Backer-Holst, T., Francis, E., & Keitch, I. (1993). *Report of the committee of inquiry into the death in Broadmoor Hospital of Orville Blackwood and a review of the deaths of two other Afro-Caribbean patients: 'Big, black and dangerous?'* London: Special Hospitals Service Authority.

Prins, H., Ashman, M., Steele, G., & Swan, M. (1998). *Report of the independent panel of inquiry into the treatment and care of Sanjay Kumar Patel*. Leicester: Leicester Health Authority.

Radford, J., & Russell, D.E.H. (eds). (1992). *Femicide: The politics of women killing*. Buckingham: Open University Press.

Reith, M. (1998). *Community care tragedies: A practice guide to mental health inquiries*. Birmingham: Venture Press (for British Association of Social Workers).

Rendell, R. (1992). *Kissing the gunner's daughter*. London: Arrow Books.

Rix, K.J.B. (1989). 'Alcohol Intoxication' or 'Drunkenness': Is there a difference? *Medicine, Science and The Law*, *29*, 100–6.

Roy, D. (1997). Clinical risk management: An emerging agenda for psychiatry. *Psychiatric Bulletin*, *21*, 162–4.

Russel, C., & Russel, W.M.S. (1961). *Human behaviour*. Boston, MA: Little Brown.

Scott, P.D. (1977). Assessing dangerousness in criminals. *British Journal of Psychiatry*, *131*, 127–42.

Smith, G. (1995). The probation service and managing dangerousness. In J. Braggins & C. Martin (eds), *Managing risk: Achieving the possible*. London: Institute for the Study and Treatment of Delinquency.

Soothill, K., & Francis, B. (1997). Poisoned chalice or just deserts?: The Sex Offenders Act 1997. *Journal of Forensic Psychiatry*, *9*, 281–93.

Stone, N. (1997). *A companion guide to life sentences*. Ilkley: Owen Wells.

Strand, S., Belfrage, H., Franson, G., & Levander, S. (1999). Clinical and risk management factors in risk prediction of mentally disordered offenders:

More important than historical data? *Legal and Criminological Psychology*, *4*, 67–76.

Street, R. (1998). *The restricted hospital order: From court to the community* (Home Office Research Study No. 186). London: Home Office Research and Statistics Directorate, Home Office.

Thompson, P., & Nelson, D. (1996). DVLA regulations concerning driving and psychiatric disorders: Knowledge and attitudes of psychiatrists. *Psychiatric Bulletin, 20*, 323–5.

Turner, M., & Kennedy, M. (1997). Tarasof and the duty to warn third parties. *Psychiatric Bulletin, 21*, 465–6.

Walker, N. (1982). Protecting People'. In J. Hinton (ed.), *Dangerousness: Problems and assessment and management*. London: Gaskell Books.

Walker, N. (1991). Dangerous Mistakes. *British Journal of Psychiatry, 158*, 752–7.

Webster, C.D., Harris, G.T., Rice, M.E., Cormier, C., & Quinsey, V.L. (1994). *The violence prediction scheme: Assessing dangerousness in high risk men*. Toronto: Centre of Criminology, University of Toronto.

West Midlands Regional Health Authority. (1991). *Report of the panel of inquiry appointed to investigate the case of Kim Kirkman*. Birmingham: Author.

Wiest, J. (1981). Treatment of violent offenders. *Clinical Social Work Journal, 9*, 271–81.

Wilson, J. (1974). *Language and the pursuit of truth*. London: Cambridge University Press.

Chapter 6

Epilogue

Never ending, still beginning

Dryden *Alexander's Feast*

During the last year or so in which I was preparing this book, NACRO's
Mental Health Advisory Committee, which I have the privilege of chair-
ing, produced a report entitled *Risk and rights: Mentally disturbed
offenders and public protection* (NACRO, 1998).[1] In this report (which
was funded by the Nuffield Foundation) we attempted to place risk
assessment in broad social and ethical contexts. We were very conscious that there had been a development of what has been called the
'risk industry' and that, as already pointed out, it had been fuelled by
media publicity and a resultant public panic. Although our efforts were
concentrated particularly on mentally disturbed offenders (including
those with psychopathic disorder) our conclusions have a general relevance to those not so diagnosed or labelled. In summary fashion, we
concluded that:

1   The great majority of mentally disturbed people do not present a
    danger to others. 'A small minority do present such a danger. This
    fact must never be allowed to dictate the overall pattern of mental
    health care, but it is important that the planning and operation of
    services take it properly into account' (p. 53).
2   There is no realistic way of removing risk entirely. To consider
    otherwise would be self-defeating, 'because additional resources
    used to contain those recognised as presenting a danger to other
    people would reduce the capacity for identifying and supporting
    potential high risk cases among other clients of mental health
    services in the community'. It would also be unjust since it would

involve placing considerable restrictions on the liberty of many mentally disturbed people, only a small proportion of whom would, in fact, be harmful to others.

3   There are dilemmas in balancing the need to protect the public on the one hand and the individual on the other, because those who are mentally disturbed are those in most serious need of care, and the risk is greatest when they do not receive that care: 'Thus, giving the most seriously disordered people the priority which their condition demands will itself tend to reduce the risk to the community at large' (p. 54).

4   The media, and through them the public, need 'to be educated to take a balanced view of the question of risk . . . and the limits of what can realistically be achieved. The most important contribution to achieving this will be made by establishing and implementing a strategy for managing risk which can be shown to be properly thought out and effective' (p. 54).

If the various chapters in this book help in any way to bring this about I shall have achieved my aims.

NOTE

1   The main work on the report was carried out on behalf of the Committee by Ian Jewesbury, Graeme Sandell and Rob Allen. The first named author was, until retirement, a senior civil servant in the Department of Health with special responsibility for mental health issues; the other two authors are senior members of NACRO's professional staff. Assistance was also provided by two additional advisors, Dr Adrian Grounds and Professor Genevra Richardson.

REFERENCE

National Association for the Care and Resettlement of Offenders. (1998). *Risk and rights: Mentally disturbed offenders and public protection: A report by NACRO's Mental Health Advisory Committee*. London: NACRO.

Name index

Subject index